Poldark's Cornwall

Poldark's Cornwall

Winston Graham

With photographs by
Simon McBride

BH

THE BODLEY HEAD
LONDON SYDNEY TORONTO

Webb & Bower
EXETER, ENGLAND

I dedicate this book
to my son and daughter,
Andrew
and
Rosamund

British Library Cataloguing in Publication Data

Graham, Winston
Poldark's Cornwall.
1. Cornwall—Description and travel
I. Title
914.23´70485   DA670.C8
ISBN 0-370-30518-3

Designed by Peter Wrigley

Text Copyright © Winston Graham 1983
Photographs Copyright © Simon McBride 1983
Design Copyright © Webb & Bower (Publishers) Limited 1983

Printed and bound in Italy for
The Bodley Head Limited
9 Bow Street, London WC2E 7AL and
Webb & Bower (Publishers) Limited
9 Colleton Crescent, Exeter, EX2 4BY
by New Interlitho SpA

Typeset in Great Britain by
Keyspools Limited, Golborne, Lancashire

First published 1983

Contents

So they all went to look,
at least as far as the stile leading
down to the beach ; further it was unsafe
to go. Where the beach would have been at any time
except the highest of tides, was a battlefield of giant waves.
The sea was washing away the lower sandhills and the
roots of marram grass. As they stood there a wave
came rushing up over the rough stony ground and
licked at the foot of the stile, leaving a trail of froth
to overflow and smear their boots. Surf in the
ordinary sense progresses from deep water to shallow,
losing height as it comes. Today waves were hitting
the rocks below Wheal Leisure with such weight
that they generated a new surf running at
right angles to the flow of the sea, with geysers
of water spouting high from the collisions.
A new and irrational surf broke against the gentler
rocks below the Long Field. Mountains of spume
collected wherever the sea drew breath, and
then blew like bursting shells across the
land. The sea was so high there was
no horizon and the clouds so low
that they sagged into
the sea.

from *The Angry Tide*

View from the North Cliffs,
looking down on to Deadman's Cove—a graveyard of many ships.
Between Portreath and St Ives.

Opposite:
Bedruthan looking towards Carnewas Island.

Early Days

I have known Cornwall since I was sixteen, and lived there thirty years before moving first to France and then to Sussex. My association with it can be divided into three phases. The first might be called the phase of delighted discovery; the second that of sun and sea addiction; the third that of nostalgic return.

*D*uring the first phase, with my first car, or more properly my mother's – one of the earliest Morris Minors – and then a Wolseley Hornet, I drove all over the county, up and down the precipitous hills, round the endless blind corners, through narrow lanes with wind-crippled hawthorn trees crouching overhead and bramble and briar clutching as we passed, into and out of grey little villages, across the scarred moorlands with the sea shimmering in the distance. And walked and walked the cliffs and the almost empty beaches, which were as yet hardly aware of their future.

Bungaloweczema, as Quiller-Couch called it, had only just begun. When the main roads were repaired, which was seldom, a new layer of tar was put on top of the old a few inches narrower each side than the last layer, so that over a period of time a steep camber built up, and two cars approaching each other on a perfectly straight road would cling to the crown until the last minute, when each would reluctantly drive with one wheel down the slope to avoid a collision. White lines and cat's eyes were of course unknown, as were 'major road ahead' signs and other amenities which make the roads curiously safer even in these congested times. I had an uncle who used to drive down annually from the north and made it his custom, he said, to go quickly across cross-roads, for that way you stood less chance of being hit. *And* he died in his bed.

Opposite above:
Bedruthan at full tide. The slight haze is thrown up by the breaking waves.

Opposite below:
Bedruthan at low tide in midsummer—bright sun, hard shadows.

Overleaf:
Rusey Beach near Crackington Haven—a dramatic volcanic landscape. The cliffs here are between four and five hundred feet high. The headland of Cambeak can be seen in the distance looking north.

Cows straying about the roads on their own, apart from milking times, were a hazard, as were horses and pigs and dogs and sheep. Although cars were a fact of life, no one really expected them in a mainly agricultural county; and anyway it was *their* business to look out.

During my first weeks of driving I attempted to thread my way with the utmost circumspection through a herd of cows going to be milked. One strolled across in front of me; I jammed on the brakes but the brakes had not been adjusted since delivery and did not work; the cow sat on the front of the car. The farmer was not concerned, neither was the cow, and the car was undamaged. At least I thought so until I came to drive home in the dark and found the headlights were squinting.

The phase of 'delighted discovery' must have lasted eight or nine years; it coincided with my earliest writing years. There was always somewhere new to go, or somewhere familiar to us but new to our friends who came in the summer. I grew to take a sort of proprietary pleasure, not only in the beauty of coves and cliffs but in the legends and the history of Cornwall.

One drive was by way of Newquay – superb beaches if you could only ignore the town – along the coast road to Watergate Bay, Bedruthan Steps and beyond. In those days caravans did not exist, except as the homes of gypsies and travelling circus hands, and although there was a small rash of new building, it was not enough to disfigure, as it disfigures now. The coast road was constantly barred by gates; a car passenger had to be deputed to hop out and open and close them. Bedruthan has one of the finest views in Cornwall: ten miles of marvellous cliff scenery and thousands of miles of water; you are looking out over the hazy rim of the world, with no land between this and Alaska. You can if you wish go down to the lonely beaches by a hundred precipitous steps: I have never felt at home at Bedruthan, never comfortable, safe. The cliffs are too high and too sheer; the beaches exist on sufferance; at the next tide they will be awash, with no dry sand to retreat to. Bathing is even more dangerous than elsewhere on the north coast. And the cliffs, though most of them have stood for millennia, have been known to fall. Of course many children these days play on the sands. It is just a personal feeling.

Not far from Bedruthan, and in sharp contrast, is the wooded Vale of Lanherne with its village of Mawgan-in-Pydar, the thirteenth-century church with a fine painted screen, and next door the old Elizabethan manor house of Lanherne, once home of the great Arundell family but a Carmelite convent for the last 190 years. You can go into the

Above:
Tin mine chimney dominating the landscape on cliffs at Zawn a Bal near Botallack.

Left:
Thrift on a stone wall – built in 'Jack and Jane' pattern.

chapel and ponder on the many famous names which have marched across the pages of Cornish history and are now no more: the Killigrews, the Bassets, the Reskymers, the Roscarrocks, the Mohuns, the Courtneys, the Trelawneys. And of these none was more important, more distinguished, more omnipresent than the Arundells – of Lanherne, of Trerice, of Tolverne, of Mendarva, of Trengwainton. Twenty of them were High Sheriffs of Cornwall. One defended Pendennis Castle for the King. Yet, as Sir Humphry Davy said as early as the beginning of the nineteenth century: 'the great stream of the Arundells of Cornwall at length like some mighty river began to lose itself among the sands as it approached the ocean shore.' Though by constant intermarriage they must have left their blood among almost all the still extant noble and landed families, the name and the estate has altogether gone from Cornwall. In the St Erme Register of 1725 the baptism of one Charles is recorded, the son of Richard Arundell, 'a day labourer'. The old house, the church and the lovely valley remain.

Another way, taking a quite opposite direction, was to go to the Roseland peninsula. It is appropriately named, though the purists say that Roseland is simply Cornish for cape. This lies on the eastern bank of the River Fal, and looks across at the busy port of Falmouth. Near St Mawes, which claims – I don't know how justly as against Penzance – the warmest climate in Britain, there is St Just-in-Roseland: a dream of a church, dating from 1261, and a dream of a churchyard sloping down the hillside to the little tidal creek below. Death to me is never anything but ugly, yet surely no one could wish a calmer, sweeter resting place than the fortunate few who share this churchyard. Its silences are always beneficent. The water slides in and out with no sound except the occasional cry of a bird; flowers line the pathways and are interspersed with granite stones bearing suitable quotations from the Bible. I am told that in the middle of the tourist rush even this haven is now deeply invaded, but I am thankful to say I have never seen it so. To me it has always been a haven of peace and tranquillity, musing the days away.

When I first saw it it was presided over by a fierce looking but in fact benevolent old rector with a white beard, who would unexpectedly as you passed come down from some ladder from which he had been inspecting the church guttering, and quote Isaiah at you. 'Beauty for ashes, the oil of joy for mourning, the garment of praise for the spirit of heaviness, that they might be called trees of righteousness, the planting of the Lord, that he might be glorified.'

Alas, he eventually lost his wife, and the big rectory was more than he could manage even with the help of Mrs

Opposite:
St Mawgan Church, Mawgan-in-Pydar near Bedruthan Steps. In the churchyard is a memorial stone to ten seamen washed ashore in 1846 at Bedruthan, frozen to death.

A winter landscape in the Roseland peninsula showing the River Fal.

Above.
The thirteenth-century church of
St-Just-in-Roseland. At full tide.

Above right :
St Mawes Castle used in the Poldark
television series as Fort Baton in
Brittany.

Saunders, the daily woman; so the Rural Dean suggested to him that a young curate might be appointed to help him, preferably a married one so that the couple should live with him in the rectory and the young wife could manage the house. This was agreed, and presently the curate and his wife arrived. They had only been married three months, and at once took to the old man and generally looked after him. But within a few weeks the young wife began to be nervous. She was convinced the vicarage was haunted and became afraid of the dark corridors, the echoing rooms, the dank chill of the house as autumn settled in and the long nights grew ever longer. She spoke to her husband about it, but he naturally pooh-poohed her fanciful notions.

It was their own bedroom – a wide, panelled room – which she found most disturbing. Curtains seemed to flap, furniture creaked. She pestered her husband to ask the old rector if the room or indeed the whole house had any reputation for being haunted, but he would not and she did not like to. Hints dropped at sewing parties and the like brought no response from her parishioners.

Then one night in the depths of the night she woke convinced there was someone or something in the bedroom. She could hear her husband's steady breathing beside her but there was another sound, another presence in the room, and close to her. Then she heard a sigh. For a few seconds she was completely frozen as if her heart was going to stop; but after a while she gathered all her courage and put out a hand towards the chair which was beside the bed on her side. Trembling, her hand touched the wooden back, groped around : there was nothing there, nothing at all. It was all some terrible nightmare. Relief growing, she allowed her hand slowly to come to rest on the seat of the chair, and the seat of the chair was warm.

This is a true story so I will not try to embellish it, but the following day the curate, having been awakened by a hysterical wife, sat at his desk wondering what sort of reason he could give to the bishop for applying for a transfer after so short a stay. Into the room came Mrs Saunders with duster but prepared to withdraw again seeing him at his desk. The curate, much troubled, and for the first time taking his wife's fears very seriously, decided to tell the daily woman all about it.

Mrs Saunders smiled: 'Lord bless you, sir, you don't want to think nothing of that! Rector's terrible lonely since Mrs died, and when he wakes up in the middle of the night and can't get off again he often goes and sits in your bedroom for company.'

The curate did not apply for a change of cure; but he bought a bedroom key.

Bessie Beneath.

On the way from Truro to St Mawes, if travelling by road and not by ferry across the Fal, you climb the long hill out of Tregony and travel south about three miles before coming to a fork in the road, right for St Just and St Mawes, left for Portloe. At this fork is a low-built granite and slate house known as Bessie Beneath. Scholars tell us this is a corruption of an old Cornish word, but sub-history in the form of tradition speaks of a Cornishwoman of good family in the seventeenth century who broke the rules of her society and

took the High Toby, i.e. turned highwayman. After terrorizing travellers for a couple of years she was shot and seriously wounded and was given shelter in this house, which was then an inn. A few weeks later she died, but, since it was a capital offence to have sheltered her, the innkeeper dared not produce her body; she was therefore buried under the slabs of the kitchen floor.

There is another Bessie in Cornwall, Bessie's Cove, near Prussia Cove. This Bessie kept an inn and was much involved with smuggling in the eighteenth century. I do not know if anyone has attempted to explain her away too.

It is quite difficult in Cornwall to take any drive without coming on cliff and coast scenery of an exceptional kind. North to Boscastle, south to St Anthony-in-Meneage, east to Fowey, west to Hell's Mouth: we took them all in those early years.

Cudden Point, Prussia Cove, where some of the early Poldark scenes were shot.

Four views of the old fishing port and mining village of Boscastle and the surrounding land and seascapes.

Left:
The harbour.

Above:
Off Boscastle harbour showing Meachard Island.

Below:
Coastal farmland in the parish of St Juliot near Boscastle.

Overleaf:
Boscastle village viewed from Penally Point.

Boscastle is still virtually unspoiled; its neighbour, Tintagel, by reason of the Arthurian legend attaching to it, overrun. It's no worse or more vulgar than Jerusalem; but to attain any sense of linkage with its mythical or semi-mythical past you have to go out of season and preferably at night when the moon is up and the wounds of cheap building are part healed by the shadows.

The district of Meneage – the second syllable pronounced to rhyme with vague – has changed refreshingly little with the years. It is not far from the Helford River but the area is sclerotic with narrow roads which lead nowhere except to these tiny villages, and development has been light. St Martin's, Manaccan – where the big old fig tree grows out of the church wall – and St Anthony, all in Meneage, are full of valerian and thatched cottages and tidal creeks and the call of birds.

Fowey too has kept its form, as John Galsworthy would have said. Possibly the lack of bathing beaches, and the early development of the old town, which at one time was the most important port on the south coast, making later building in the restricted area by the river more difficult, has helped. For this reason and others it is of all Cornish coastal towns the least changed. Yet it gives the impression of being more Victorian than mediaeval, as if Quiller-Couch's spirit still hangs over it, preserving it in the mould he set.

I found Hell's Mouth when I visited it recently less impressive than I used to – perhaps because of the wooden fencing which now preserves tourists from taking that dangerous last step to peer over, perhaps because apart from its name there are other and more dramatic cliffs along the same coast.

★ ★ ★

Opposite:
The author on Perranporth Beach. In the background is the wooden bungalow he rented and walked to each day to write the novel *Demelza*.

And in the winter when the season was over and the visitors were gone, the residents left behind were relatively few. The population of Cornwall did not materially increase between 1840 and 1940 and was never as much as the modern city of Bristol, a number varying – down as well as up – between 300,000 and 350,000 spread over an area of 1350 square miles. The rush of the short busy season would leave one, when it was over, feeling peculiarly alone, and relishing that loneliness. Then one became more than ever a part of the shouting winds and the oceanic seas which interspersed in winter months with still days of brilliant sunshine and weeping days of endless misty rain.

Where we lived then, a mile from the village of Perranporth, we had no electricity, no piped water, no telephone.

Above:
Godrevy Lighthouse from Upton Towans.

Right:
The walk northwards from Godrevy Point towards
Navax Point and Hell's Mouth. The shortage of
good arable land results in cultivation of the land to
the extreme edge of the cliffs.

The bungalow in which we lived was one of only three put up by a speculative builder; and so the three stayed, isolated, for a number of years, like pustules, early symptoms of a dread disease. Now Perrancombe has died of it. But in those days the dark and muddy lane from the village was lit, at appropriate seasons, only by the green glimmer of glow-worms or made noisy with the love-sawings of crickets.

I was born and bred in Manchester, in Victoria Park, a residential park with bars like customs barriers at all the entrances to keep out 'undesirables'. At some date the barriers fell and it is now, I am told, almost a slum; but in those days it laid some claim to its name by reason of the numerous trees growing there. I still have pressed in a *Primer of Biology & Nature Study* belonging to my father leaves of the oak, lime, birch, elm, chestnut, ash, hornbeam and larch that I collected and put between the pages when I was nine and first developed an interest in such things. But, since this enclave was only three miles from the centre of the city, young leaves were soon darkened by deposits from the not so distant chimneys of industry, and most of the foliage came to look heavy and depressed, particularly as the summer wore on, and fell early.

The vegetation of the north Cornish coast could hardly have been more different. Trees – there were hardly any trees at all as I knew them. Nothing, of course, near the sea. Even valleys such as Perrancombe could only boast a few wind-tortured elms. A thicket of hawthorns would slant at an angle of forty degrees as if sliced by a giant Flymo. To persuade an ordinary common *Cupressus macrocarpa* to endure a few seasons was an achievement. But the undergrowth was altogether different. This rampaged and flourished everywhere. The hedges, the verges, the commons, the railway banks, were choked with weeds, which in their season became wild flowers. In the spring campion and milkmaids and bluebells fought with each other in patriotic colour, disputing their ground with fern and bracken and gorse and cow parsnip and wild garlic and a dozen other rivals for a place in the rain and the sun. Some years the gorse would be so outrageous as to hurt the eye.

It has by no means all gone, of course. Only that the riot has been much subdued wherever mechanical hedge-clipping machines can operate. And many gorse commons have been taken for building or cultivation.

Reared as I was on a diet of geraniums, marguerites, and a few tired roses and sweet peas, I also found the variety of garden plants that would grow in this shallow, sandy soil endless and exciting. Almost all the ordinary garden plants were quite new to me: plants that I would hardly bother with

Opposite above:
Hell's Mouth where many ships have been wrecked.

Opposite below:
North Cliffs looking towards Crane Islands near Portreath.

now, such as calendula, scabious, eschscholtzia, cheiranthus, tree lupins, *Bellis perennis*, arabis, clarkia, sweet william; they all grew with the vigour of weeds and flowered extravagantly. Perhaps fortunately at that stage I had not visited the special gardens on the south coast with their huge semi-tropical flowers and trees which in their season are the most exotic and beautiful I have seen anywhere in the world. Once you have seen a 30-foot *Magnolia mollicomata* in full bloom at Caerhays nothing about gardens is ever quite the same again.

To walk down the combe and up the hill to the cliffs to watch the rough seas at Droskyn was a constant pleasure. Before I ever saw Cornwall, as a boy on holiday on the Lancashire coast, where the tides are not to be despised, I would spend just as long as I was allowed standing in the teeth of the wind watching, and if necessary dodging, the great seas as they came over the sea walls. Cornwall has no walls but the natural, and of course much more beautiful, walls of granite. It also has in many places grotesque rock formations which

Above:
Chapel Rock at Perranporth, or Chapel Angarder as it was originally called. It once belonged to the ancient manor of Reen, and a small Christian chapel was sited on it.

Opposite:
Perranporth Beach at low tide. Gull Rocks (originally called Carter's Rocks) are in the distance. The gulls use the rocks as a permanent resting place.

Overleaf:
Penwith moors near Bosporthennis.

Above:
At the entrance of Blue Hills Mine, Trevellas.

Top:
Wild flowers on North Cliffs below Reskajeage Downs.

Left:
Wild flowers at West Pentire with Porth Joke in the distance.

have been man-made. Droskyn is a maze of holes and arches, most of them created by hardy tinners of the past, men in search of profit who for once, and quite inadvertently, have added to the picturesqueness of a place instead of destroying it. You go down to the Droskyn sands – when there are any – by way of a narrow ravine or gully. This was originally a tunnel driven by the pilchard seiners who used to keep their boats down there in the summer and haul them up through the tunnel to safety during the winter. One wet October the tunnel fell in and the ravine was created.

There used to be four pilchard fishing companies in Perranporth alone; 'The Union', 'Miners', 'Farmers', and 'The Love'. Considering that the village never had any sort of harbour and was exposed to a lee shore, this was a fair testimony to the hardiness of the fishermen (who were also often miners as well).

A good walk when the weather was not too wild was to Wheal Prudence, a long-extinct copper mine on the cliffs in the direction of St Agnes. This is Cornwall at its wildest; cliffs as high as Bedruthan but with no paths down and virtually no shore. A great breeding place for gulls, and a place to gather gulls' eggs. This is what the gulls think, for they try to scare you away by dive-bombing you. Altogether gathering them is a perilous business, not from the gulls but from the risk of losing one's grip and slipping 300 feet into the sea. A man and his wife did just that at this place in June 1834, though they were not after eggs but samphire, a cliff plant which at the time was much used in Cornwall for cooking and as a pickle. As Edgar says in *King Lear*: 'Half way down hangs one that gathers samphire; dreadful trade.' Dreadful trade, indeed. Poor Mark Thomas and his wife would have agreed with him, but they had four children to support and no other livelihood.

Two miles further along this cliff path you come down into Trevellas Porth and the Blue Hills Mine. This is virtually untouched, unrepaired, undeveloped from the days of mining prosperity, and illustrates the desolation caused in the high noon of the industry, in the 1840s and 50s, by the dumping of attle, or mining refuse. People who criticize what Perran-porth has now become – and I am first among them – might have thought little more highly of it a hundred odd years ago when, apart from the few houses, all available free space had

Cornish fishermen row out on a dawn tide.
The oars give more control in the breaking waves than the engines they
use to reach the Runnel Stone fishing grounds. The traditional catch of
pilchards has now been replaced by mackerel.

Above:
The Strangles—Samphire Rock.

Right:
Between Perranporth and St Agnes
below Wheal Prudence.

Opposite:
The jetty at Sennen Cove.

Above:
The three-hundred-year-old Pilchard
Store at Penberth Cove.

Above left:
Sennen Cove fishermen mending nets.

Left:
A pilchard fisherman's cottage with a
cobbled floor at Penberth Cove.

Above:
St Ives Bay at dawn.

Left:
Mackerel fishermen in Penberth Cove.

Below:
A fisherman packing his catch of mackerel in Penberth Cove.

been used as a dump for mineral waste piled higher than the houses and encroaching on every field and track. That it was ever moved was thanks to the decision to build a New Road across to Bolingey and the estuary of the once-tidal marshes, which accepted more and more of the mineral refuse before it ever became firm enough to take a cart or a bus.

Even when I first lived there the scars had not all gone. The garden of our first house was richly green, but soil deeper than four inches did not exist. This area had been used for washing floors, and all except a thin veneer of newly laid soil had been washed away. The second house we had was built on a beautiful raised site, which consisted, we later found, of mineral deposits from a mine worked a quarter of a mile away. An attempt to grow potatoes on this ground during World War II was laughable. The grass tennis courts in the centre of the village were and are the best drained in England. Nor was it altogether unknown in the village for holes to appear in the middle of the night because of a belated collapse underground. On one occasion a young man recently come to live in a cottage in the middle of the village decided to split some kindling wood on the lime ash floor in front of the kitchen stove, when after a few strokes the floor gave way and block, stick and hatchet disappeared into the adit waterway tunnelled below.

In undeveloped land near the bungalow where I first lived a tin-stamp still worked, fed by a leat which was a diversion from the stream that ran at the foot of our garden. Half a mile away water had been split from the main stream and, part contained in a ditch, part running between sealed wooden linings, it worked two or three stamps before rejoining the parent stream. Of these all had gone except the last one just beyond our house. That is to say the water passed *above* our bungalow on the other side of the road, at least twelve feet higher than the main stream, and, a hundred yards further on, it ran under the road and was allowed to fall over a waterwheel, and by so doing activated the iron crushing heads that broke up the ore tipped here from a neighbouring mine. The water then worked a couple of circular washing floors before being permitted to rejoin the main stream.

Night and day the bizarre thumping went on. In windy weather one hardly noticed it. On still moonlit nights it was like the tread of manacled giants. When I walked up the valley in the dark it was the loneliest sound I've ever heard.

After I was married this piece of land came up for sale, and so that no one should build next to my mother's bungalow, I bought it. By now the stamps were a ruin, the wheels aslant, the iron rods rusty and long silent. One day a young man with a dark complexion and a pointed beard called on me and asked

Opposite:
Tredinnick Mine on Bosullow Common in Penwith district.

Left:
Blue Hills Mine. The main engine
house at the bottom of Trevellas
Porth.

Above:
Detail of a wall of the engine house.

Overleaf:
Blue Hills Mine.

Above:
Towanroath shaft, Wheal Coates,
Chapel Porth.

Left:
Basset's Cove near Portreath.

Above:
A fifty-fathom shaft.

Above right:
Repairing a track.

Right:
A mineworker from Geevor.

Far right:
A miner working on a stope. 'A
Stope – when a pit is sunk down in a
lode they break and work it away, as
it were, in stairs or steps, one man
following another and breaking the
ground, which manner of working in
a sump is called stoping and that
height or step which each man
breaks is called a stope.'
Dr William Pryce, 1778,
from *Mineralogia Cornubiensis*.

me if I owned the 'stamps land' up Perrancombe, and, by association, the stamps. I said I did. He explained that he was operating a small tin mine entirely on his own at Mithian and that parts of the wheel and the heads and lifters would be useful to him. Could he buy them? Although reluctant to part with this picturesque ruin I agreed that he could have them, and at no cost to himself except the transport. He was pleased at this and we chatted a few minutes in the autumn sunshine. He was upset at the way Cornwall was getting spoiled, and felt it was largely the result of up-country folk coming to the county and developing it for their own profit. He also expressed a grudge against up-country writers who came here and wrote about the county and made money out of it all. Interested in this remark, I asked him if he had any particular writers in mind. He replied: 'Well, this chap Winston Graham, for instance.'

A quicker-witted man would no doubt have led him on; instead I blurted out my guilt at once. He did not see this as amusing, but neither was he at all embarrassed. After a few

Right:
A miners' tunnel at St Agnes near
Hanover Cove.

Overleaf:
Botallack. Shallow deposits of tin
were sometimes found in the form of
floors, one beneath another. The
best known of these was the 'Bunny'
at Botallack, which was almost level
with the surface. The tin stone was
first discovered by horses kicking it
up as they went over it. Below this
was a floor of 'country' 1–3 feet
thick, then a second floor of tin, then
another floor of 'country', and so on
until seven floors of tin were
uncovered. The thickness of each
was from 6–12 feet, and some were
30 feet in diameter.

seconds of thoughtful staring he explained accusatively that he lived at Mingoose, and that since the early Poldark novels were published he had been much troubled by people coming around looking for Mingoose House, where in the novels the Treneglos family lives. 'They come round my place Sat'day af'noons, Sunday mornings, looking for Mingoose House. There isn't no Mingoose House. There isn't no such place. Tis a proper nuisance!'

However, after I had apologized again for being who I was, he came to take a more favourable view of me. Had I ever been down a one-man mine? No, I said. 'Then come Sunday af'noon, I'll show ee.' Which he did. It was clearly part of an old mine which he had redeveloped. The ladders were shaky and so in the end was I. Later we went back to his cottage for tea, and he played me hymn tunes on the organ he had built himself into the wall of the cottage.

A character – and Cornwall is rich in characters. All this happened ages ago, but I have recently turned this encounter to use by making him the model for Ben Carter.

Incidentally I still own the piece of land – still known as the 'stamps land' – and it is now the only piece of rough undeveloped ground remaining in Perrancombe.

A moorland farmer on Bosullow Common near Pendeen, during the annual hedge-cutting by hand.

Above: Spring tide at Treyarnon.

Opposite:
The Strangles and Voter Run from High Cliff.
Beeny Cliff is the distant headland.

Cornish Sea

The second phase – that of sun and sea addiction – merged imperceptibly and gradually overtook the first. It is, if analysed, a rather mindless addiction: no great philosophies, as far as I know, were ever evolved on a beach; few penetrating thoughts or illuminating ideas cross one's mind when one's body is grilling in the sun. It is essentially a pagan occupation and therefore very suitable to the people of our time. Certainly no one since the Druids has paid so much attention to the sun as we have: it has assumed its place as a secular god to which hordes of the human race offer annual tribute. The debatable assumption that one is in better health if one's skin is tanned, is offset by the not at all debatable fact that one *looks* better.

So I admit this addiction with due acknowledgement of its inutility but without apology. An intellectual friend of mine once described Contract Bridge as 'systematized frittering'. Sitting in the sun seems to me to be a sort of benign frittering without any system at all.

Cornish sunshine has one of the highest tanning capacities in the world. You can get browner after a week in Cornwall than after three in Nice. (Always supposing the sun is shining in Cornwall, which naturally is a considerable supposition.) People account for this by speaking of the wind; but it is probably more than that; the air is so light that ultraviolet rays pass through it more intensely. I have often seen newly arrived friends sitting in the sun and turning colour while I watched, like litmus paper.

But of course to go with the sun there has to be sea. Without it the sun is oppressive, headachy, tiring. With the close proximity of the sea all that is changed. And for me it must be salt water: the modern cult of the swimming pool seems symptomatic of this ersatz age. Bathing or body surfing – particularly the latter – on the north coast under a hot Cornish sun is an experience hundreds of thousands of people now come every year to savour for themselves.

Body surfing has now been partly superseded by wind surfing and the cult of the Malibou. But it is still the most popular and the most frequently indulged in – and I suspect the most enjoyable, because one's body is almost entirely submerged in water without benefit of wet suits. To catch a really successful wave is a very peculiar pleasure and a thrill. To come in on a wave on the north coast when a south easterly wind is blowing, riffling the lips of the waves as they topple, is like being propelled landwards at great speed in a soda siphon world.

In a summer of long ago, after a shaky start, the weather set fair on the 9th July, and thereafter the sun shone brilliantly every day until late September. We picnicked each day without fail. My wife's hand wore out with cutting sandwiches. Though I had her and two children to support, and in those days only lived from novel to novel, I confined myself to two hours' work in the mornings and swore to make it up when the autumn came or the weather broke. (One of the disadvantages of fine weather in England is that one has to snatch at it while it is there and never, never rely on tomorrow.)

So throughout that summer we picnicked and sun-bathed and surfed and gradually turned more and more nigger-brown. Came a terrible week in August when business took me to London. I thundered off to Truro, after a last picnic, to catch the night train, hurried round my appointments, and after six days went rushing home inescapably convinced that the weather would have broken in my absence. It had not. The same pale sky and paler, pellucid sea, the same unremittingly glorious sun.

It was the year my son went to his public school and we had to leave with him on the 18th September. The 17th was largely taken up with preparations and packing, but in the early evening we escaped onto Perranporth beach on an

Right:
Perranporth Beach.

Overleaf:
Penhalt Cliff near Widemouth Bay, south of Bude.

incoming tide. There was no wind and the sun was hot but it was a huge sea. One was reminded of Tennyson's:

> Nine large piles of troubled water
>   Turbulently come;
> From the bosom of his mother,
> Each one leaping on his brother,
>   Scatters lusty foam.
>
> In the sky a wondrous silence,
>   Cloud-surf, mute and weird;
> In the distance, still uplifting,
> Ghostly fountains vanish, drifting,
>   Like a Druid's beard.

It was one of those seas when a surfer catches one wave, is borne along a dizzying way, then dropped upon another, and so upon another, and even sometimes on a fourth. As we staggered together out of the sea joyfully exhausted after our fifteenth such run, my son said to me: 'Daddy, people who have never done this haven't lived.' He was not far wrong.

So the second phase went on and on. A wet day or a dull day in the summer was a day for work; on a good day most of the ordinary attractions of Cornwall were ignored in our rush to one of our three or four most prized beaches.

To Towan, near Portscatho on the south coast (when the wind or sea was unfavourable on the north, or there was sea fog). Or to near-by Porthcurnick, where eminently upsettable floats could be hired. And on the north coast most often to Treyarnon or to West Pentire, near Crantock.

Towan is a lovely small, rock and sand beach where there is no surf but endless brilliant rock pools, seaweed grown, anemone starred and full of tiny fishes and shells. It is also one of the few places in Cornwall where cowries can be found. The cliffs gently slope, green almost to the sea. And there are no houses of any sort. When we left Cornwall it was just beginning to be spoiled. Caravans encroached on the sandy field leading down to the cove. There were a few more every year. It was only a matter of time before an ice-cream kiosk came and a hut hiring out deck chairs and selling teas.

For a reason I cannot now remember it was five or six years before we returned to it, dreading what we might find. What we found was all the caravans gone, an arrow pointing to a fairly distant car park, and the one or two people on the beach outnumbered by the Friesian cows which sat around chewing by the water's edge. We rubbed our eyes. This was an instance of the clock being put *back*! How could it be?

Opposite above:
The Red River at Gwithian, the colour being caused by the outflow from copper mines.

Opposite below:
Padstow taken from the far bank of the River Camel near Rock.

Above:
South of St Agnes Head at Tubby's Head below
St Agnes Beacon.

Left: The gorse on West Pentire.

Above:
A rockpool below Treyarnon Point.

Right:
Constantine Bay—wind in the marram grass.

A field of wheat at Porth Joke.

The answer was in fact simple. The National Trust had got it.

What we in England, and people in Cornwall especially, owe to the National Trust is beyond computation.

There are, of course, two separate functions which the National Trust performs. One is the preservation of land, the other of houses. As to the second of these purposes, my feelings are, I have to say, a little ambivalent. Of course when a family finds itself unable to continue to maintain a vast property it has inherited, a take-over of this sort is probably better than any other solution which offers. And sometimes when the family continues in part possession and lives in the house as before it can work well enough. But when the owners go the houses die. I think particularly of Trerice, near Newquay, the house I used as a model for Trenwith, where the main family of the Poldarks lived. This superb small Elizabethan house, with its magnificent hall and gracious drawing room, was built by a branch of the Arundell family in 1572 and 3. There was competition between them and the Arundells of Lanherne as to which was the senior branch, but there can be little doubt that the Arundells of Trerice built the more beautiful house. It was from here that old Sir John Arundell, aged then about seventy-five, rode out to defend Pendennis Castle against the Parliamentary army of Fairfax in 1646, and to hold it for five months – this being the last place in England, except for Raglan, to fly the standard of the King.

I remember Trerice when it was privately owned. I remember an occasion of a party with candles and big fires blazing and music from the minstrel gallery. Now it is a shell: neat, excellently kept, with a capacious car park and a little shop. Just after World War II it was offered to me for £12,000.

Another such house is Trelissick – which I mention under its own name in the Poldark novels – a splendid medium-size pillared eighteenth-century mansion built in the valley going down to King Harry Ferry with swardy fields and woodlands overlooking the River Fal. This too has become one of the properties owned by the National Trust. I believe the owners still use it at times, but with the inevitable car park, the café, the large garden centre, the signs *way in, way out, ladies, gents,* etc., it can only approximate to the house I knew when the previous generation lived there throughout the year and its privacy was unassailed.

But in some cases where the presence is less obtrusive the partnership comes off. Such is St Michael's Mount, where private ownership continues uninterrupted – and un-interfered with – by the visitors that the Mount attracts.

Opposite above:
Trerice Manor, used as a model for Trenwith in the Poldark novels.

Opposite below:
The Great Hall at Trerice.

Namphillows Wood at Trelissick.

Above:
The village of Flushing on the
River Fal.

Right:
Trelissick House, the home of
Ralph-Allen Daniell in the Poldark
novels.

St Michael's Mount was of course for centuries a priory for the Benedictine monks, but it has been the subject of siege and counter-siege by secular and semi-secular armies on and off for the last eight hundred years. Disaffection sprang from here, from Perkin Warbeck to the Prayer Book Rebellion; and loyalty, as in its adherence to the King's Cause, in Stuart days. The Bassets of Tehidy owned it during the critical years of the struggle between Cavalier and Roundhead, were impoverished as a result of Cromwell's triumph, and sold it to the St Aubyns, of Clowance in the parish of Crowan, who, when the monarchy was restored, somehow contrived, as others did, like General Monck, to compound their dissidencies and to hold on to their possessions. It has been in the same family ever since.

For centuries it had been regarded as little more than a summer home by the families owning it, but a hundred years ago an entirely new wing was built alongside and underneath the original castle. So ingeniously was this done that a new house was added without altering the sky-line or much of the

Above:
The square-rigged sailing ship *The Marques* used in the second Poldark series, anchored at St Michael's Mount.

Overleaf:
St Michael's Mount from Perranuthnoe at sunrise.

over-all appearance; and today it is quite hard to distinguish between the Victorian and the twelfth-century granite. Thus the St Levans – they were ennobled in 1887 – are able to live a private life while thousands of visitors annually pass around the church and the old castle just above. Piers St Aubyn, the architect, whose restorations of churches in Cornwall were to say the least not notably successful, can hardly have realized how successfully, and in this case how tastefully, he was designing for the future.

So much for the houses. But however successful or unsuccessful the adoption of this or that house has been, there can be nothing but admiration and gratitude for the National Trust's ownership of land. The fate from which Towan has been saved is a tiny sample of what so much of the Cornish coast has been preserved from by this marvellous organization. Look at an Ordnance Survey map of Cornwall and see those blessed initials N. T. in red appearing and reappearing at intervals all the way from Bude to Land's End and from Land's End to Plymouth. (Land's End itself, as we know, does not belong to them.) So much of the splendid cliff land and seascape has been saved from development in perpetuity.

Of course the campers and the trippers and the exploiters are everywhere they can get, but there are now so many areas where they cannot get – or can only get to leave alone, or to appreciate, which many of them do just as much as you or I. Lured by television when *Poldark* was being made, I went to a district new to me: Pentireglaze near Lundy Bay, which is itself not very far from Polzeath, and found an area which could hardly have changed in a century. The only concession was a two-foot-wide cliff path winding its way among the wild flowers, and a few – very few – people wandering along it delighting in the view.

Opposite:
The Lundy Bay area where Ross broke down the Warleggan fence in the second Poldark television series.

Left:
Pentireglaze. Used in the second Poldark television series for the scene with Hugh Armitage and Demelza.

One thing in passing here I will say for television crews: they may occupy a site for three days, the number of people involved being probably thirty or forty, and when they have gone you will not find a can, a cigarette packet, a cigar stub, a toffee paper or a cork. It would be so nice if ordinary holiday-makers were like this.

To return to my addiction and our two favourite places on the north coast. Treyarnon is north of Bedruthan Steps and is a fine bay but is dominated by an enormous car park. And though building over the years has been minimal the caravans surround it now in great numbers. It is quite clearly exploited, but it would be difficult, unless one were spoil-sport enough to prohibit visitors altogether, to see how to prevent this. The sands are good for children, there is a natural rock swimming pool, the surf is unbeatable.

We used to try to reach Treyarnon about low tide. Half an hour to an hour after that, when the tide was just beginning to make, you could get fantastic waves; not such long runs as a beach like Perranporth, but one could stand knee-deep in water and see the monstrous green cavern turn above one's head, and then be engulfed and tossed towards the shore like a cork, shouting one's head off with excitement. This operation was somewhat safer with a short rubber li-lo such as they use in South Africa rather than the normal wooden board of Cornwall; but many hardy spirits, including all my family except myself, stuck to the wooden board. This operation would nowadays of course be altogether forbidden – no doubt rightly – by the Surf Guards, whose duty it is to save foolhardy people from taking too much risk in enjoying themselves – or leading the less experienced on.

Above:
The sea boiling at Treyarnon.

Above left:
Treyarnon Beach.

But the fourth of the four beaches was the one to which we went most often: West Pentire. Here the surf is more chancy – you have to pick and choose your time to catch it and even then, if straying, may come at odds with the Surf Guards – but a narrow cove there offers the perfect sun trap and is protected from everything except a south-east wind. It is a fine beach at low tide and the cove forms a rock-fringed swimming pool when the tide comes in. Other smaller pools, refilled each tide, are constantly fished by small boys and their fathers during the summer months, and thin white legs stalk and paddle in and out of the water, examining the sea anemones, the crabs, and the fishes built like spectral shrimps which dart in and out of the gently waving weed. Northerly winds, a natural accompaniment to a certain type of fine weather in Cornwall, may whistle overhead and make the rest of the county shiver – but this cove is protected from them. Sometimes, and not infrequently, you bask in drowsy sun while monumental clouds hover over the rest of Cornwall. It is a charmed spot.

It was this cove, and the headland that juts out beyond it making the western claw of Crantock Bay, and the further bay beyond of Porth Joke – or Polly Joke, as it is known locally – which helped most to make up a composite picture of the Nampara of the Poldark novels. Nothing, of course, is exactly right. If I describe a town in the eighteenth century – Truro or Redruth or Falmouth – it is I hope as accurately described as if you had in front of you a town map of the time. But the north coast – and Nampara and St Ann's and Sawle – are all composite pictures giving the right impression but seldom keeping to exact topographical detail. Hendrawna Beach is more like Perranporth Beach than Crantock Bay. Wheal Leisure is not where it really was – in the centre of Perranporth village – but out near Wheal Vlow, beyond Flat Rocks, and Nampara is most like an old manor farm in the parish of St Endellion, miles to the north. (This house was actually used as Nampara for the second series of *Poldark* on television.)

But it was West Pentire where I spent so much of my time; watching the flickering colours in the water; the white flash of gulls' wings, angular and sharp, against slanting skies; the sea pinks clinging perpendicularly to the gentler rocks like close-cropped pink beards; the thump of waves forcing their way through a blow hole and turning spume into mist; the welter of wild flowers in the unspoiled fields: stonecrops, corn-flowers, scabious, celandines, primroses, bluebells, violets, campions, ox-eye daisies, cow parsley, bladderwort, ladies' fingers and the rest; the flat almost slaty rocks that slid quietly by steps into the sea at the point's end; the endless procession

Opposite above:
The author at Porth Joke.

Opposite below:
The harbour side at Falmouth. 'This town of Falmouth, as you will partly conjecture, is no great ways from the sea. It is defended on the sea side by two castles, St Maws and Pendennis, extremely well calculated for annoying everybody except the enemy. St Maws is garrisoned by an able-bodied person of four score, a widower. He has the whole command and sole management of six most unmanageable pieces of ordnance, admirably adapted for the destruction of Pendennis, a like tower of strength on the opposite side of the Channel. The town contains many Quakers and salt fish – the oysters having a taste of copper, owing to the soil of the mining country – the women (blessed be the corporation therefor!) are flogged at the cart's tail when they pick and steal, as happened to one of the fair sex yesterday noon. She was pertinacious in her behaviour and damned the mayor.' From a letter written by Lord Byron, at Falmouth, dated 25th June, 1809.

Above:
A waterfall of moss at West Pentire.

Above right:
A gull on a Cornish rock.

of cloud and sun against the background of the wide skies.

It was here I came many times as a youth before World War II; and it was here I walked often with the girl I was going to marry, thrushing through the low surf a mile across the beach and back, planning our honeymoon – which never came off because of the outbreak of war. Five years later, when it was all over, we returned, and picked and hacked our way down the overgrown paths, slashing at nettles and brambles, and negotiating as best we could the fences of barbed wire, reaching at last our beloved cove. It was untouched, unchanged: there might have been no war, no bloodshed, no terror, no hatred, no torture, no genocide, no Belsens, no Stalingrads, no Hiroshimas. The sea was just creeping round the corner of the cove, a ripple advancing over the dry sand, retreating again as if not sure. A rivulet of fresh water dripped from the rocks; the rock from which it fell was a curtain of green moss; the tiny stream a few inches wide trickled out across the sand to greet the sea. A large herring gull, feet planted primly on a nearby rock, eyed us askance. He had become unused to such intrusion.

We had returned. We have been returning ever since.

★ ★ ★

*S*ince this is not an autobiography it is no proper place for explaining my reasons for leaving Cornwall. Yet something must be said to introduce the advent of the third phase.

A writer is an odd bird, and often does not reason like other people. As I became more and more successful it seemed to me that I was becoming too comfortable too young. Everything slotted into place so easily. I was happily married, my two children were prospering at their public schools; we travelled abroad a couple of times a year, once with the children, once on our own. I spent a week in London every two months. I was successful and set. No doubt that ugly word Ambition nudged at my elbow. If one doesn't have ambition to write better at that age, it is a poor look-out. Whatever the cause, I became convinced that to move would broaden my outlook. I did not want to become known as a regional novelist. I did not want to become known as a historical novelist. I did not want to become known as a crime novelist. I just wanted to be a novelist. So we moved.

A friend of mine, a well-known writer – much better known than I am – decided, possibly for similar reasons, to make such a change. In the course of six months he changed his place of residence, his club, his publisher, his agent, and his wife. I only changed my place of residence.

My reason, after a year in France, for settling in Sussex was that I have two other areas which are of great and enduring interest to me. One is London and one is France, and my present house is forty-eight miles from one and twenty from the other (at least to the car-ferry). Unfortunately it is much too far (250–300 miles of abominable undeveloped roads) from my third and most abiding interest. But one of my main reasons for not jolting myself again – this time into a return to Cornwall – is the fact that my wife's asthma is so much better in a drier climate.

So . . . the third phase of a long relationship with Cornwall has begun and endured. In the main it has consisted of visits – once to three times a year – usually in high summer, when, if the weather has been good we have simply gone flying to one of our favourite spots, and spent all day there, returning to our hotel or rented house only when the sun was losing its heat and clouds were drifting up over the sea. But in the nature of English weather, and especially Cornish weather, grey days and wet days are more common than fine; and, unlike one's reactions when *living* in a place, when the natural tendency on such days is to stay in, on holiday one feels obliged to go out; and so many new trips have come about, rediscovering old places, surprising oneself with new.

This has been particularly so in the last seven or eight years since *Poldark* has been done on TV. Production managers in television, I might mention, don't take kindly to advice. They believe that they and/or their scouts know Cornwall better than you do; better, in fact, than anyone else does; and the only way of getting them to adopt one of the locations you want them to use is to make them think they thought of it first.

Yet allied to this unadmirable trait are the admirable ones of drive and total dedication, and a determination almost literally to leave no stone unturned in a search for the suitable site. Nor are they in any way inhibited by a fear of intruding on anyone's privacy: after all, the magic word 'television' is enough to melt the indignation of almost anyone feeling they are being intruded upon. So they explore the possibilities of old manors jealously guarded by their owners from public gaze; they discover gorse-fringed coves to which there is no access except across ploughed fields; they interview farmers and vicars and take tea with noblemen and old ladies. They enlist the help of the Ministry of Works, the Dock Board, the police, the RAF, and any and every other organization private or public which they think may conceivably come in useful to the unit. And all in the name of that one holy word.

And in the course of doing all this they discover – for themselves and for others who happen to be involved – hidden corners of Cornwall that would scarcely ever otherwise come to light.

So it has been with me.

Additionally, when you live in Cornwall you are rooted in a home, and that home has a location which, while not exactly restricting the car driver, is returned to each night. The result is you come to know your own area best. On the other hand, if you don't live in Cornwall and over a number of years come to stay in a succession of differently located hotels, you discover these different areas better than you have ever done before. This has been particularly true for me of parts of east Cornwall and of the country west of Penzance.

Living where we now do, we often when going to Cornwall drive to London and take the overnight Motorail, Paddington to Penzance. This is a very uncomfortable journey. It was said of Jimmy 'Schnozzle' Durante, the American comedian, that, when on one occasion he had to go out at five o'clock in the morning on some mission or other, he was seen to be viciously slapping the boles of the trees he passed. Asked what he was doing he replied: 'When I'm awake, no boid sleeps.' This seems to be the principle of all British Rail train drivers on this run. No start is ever made without the maximum jerk, no stop without a bone-shaking jolt. And since the train on its way wanders up into the backyards of Bristol, there is ample opportunity for both.

Above:
The green tranquil area round Mount's Bay.

Left:
Penzance with the Church of St Mary.

Penzance at low tide.

But by about seven the sleeping pill and the night's epilepsies are working off together, and the train seems to have recovered its temper and to be running more gently, more easily downhill towards the end of England. Without sliding the window back you can almost guess where you are. Increasing speed and two tunnels, and then the viaduct before Truro, the bulk of the great cathedral turning, dominating the town, the new day glinting off the granite, the single copper spire greener than ever before; then the gloom of Truro station. All this horribly nostalgic: this was the end of so many of my journeys home when I lived in Cornwall; greeted on the station by a wife and two excited children, flying home in the open Alvis laughing and chattering towards the sea.

Those days are now gone; the train starts again, pattering easily through the treeless, valleyed countryside; grey houses, gaunt mine-shafts; a few early cars speeding along the new roads, cattle idly staring, bits of gorse still out; we stop, quite gently now, at little grey stations. The sky is heavily

loaded but streaks of sunlight promise better things to come. All the old names: Redruth, Camborne, Hayle, St Erth; then the long straight run along the causeway, with the Mount rising like a mirage from the quiet sea. Slowly at last we creep into Penzance. We pick up our night bag, carry it the length of the platform to where the car, spirited ahead by another train, is waiting. The sun is now full out; the weather may altogether clear; for us breakfast at the Queen's and then the whole long day ahead.

A moorland farm in the Penwith peninsula with a typical wall dividing the fields.

★ ★ ★

The Celtic language was in retreat from eastern Cornwall before the Norman Conquest. The Anglo-Saxons had been in control of these areas for some centuries before they themselves were overwhelmed by the Normans and William I sent his half-brother, Robert Count of Mortain, to build Launceston Castle and from there oversee the conquered lands. (Sir Henry de Tyes was lord of the Nampara area on the north coast.) But the gradual withdrawal of the Celtic ethos farther and farther west, if not a resistance to conquest, was at least a resistance to the submergence of Celtic ways and traditions, and took two-thirds of a millennium to complete. Not until 1777 did the last woman die who spoke Cornish as her native tongue, and she, fittingly, lived in Paul near Mousehole. Nowadays there is a strong movement to revive the language. The effort has my sympathy but not much more. Having spent a lifetime struggling to understand and make myself understood in half the languages of Europe – and mostly failing for I am a very poor linguist – I cannot see much advantage in adding yet another tongue for children to learn. Unlike Welsh and Irish, the Cornish language has little valuable literature of its own; and sentiment and nostalgia are not enough.

I have much more sympathy for the demand for a greater control of local government. I would like, for instance, Cornwall to have the power to levy an extra annual tax on every caravan situated permanently in the county, and on every caravan entering it.

But the Celtic retreat has been at its slowest from Penzance westward. Even the land is different. At almost the farthest west, the Assyrian cliffs of Tol-Pedn-Penwith – much more impressive than Land's End – lead down to the fishing hamlet of Porthgwarra, known for its Runnel Stone lobsters and the tunnels driven through the granite to reach the shore. (We spent a day of our part-cancelled honeymoon fishing off the Runnel Stone and eating ham sandwiches, to the surprise of our boatman who clearly expected us to lose our appetite if nothing else as we lurched and eddied round that fashionable graveyard of ships.)

At the end of the road half a mile from Porthcurno is the Church of St Levan. It is said that no one has ever been christened Joanna there, because in the seventh century the saint was one day going down to his fishing place below the church and was rebuked by a woman called Joanna for doing this on a Sunday. He replied that this was no more of a sin than was her activity in picking pot-herbs from her garden. The woman was obdurate and the argument grew heated: St Levan called her Foolish Joanna and went on his way with the comment that if another of her name was so christened she would turn out a bigger fool than the woman confronting him. Thereafter any parents in the parish wishing to call their daughter Joanna have carried her over to Sennen.

Nearby is the Minack Theatre, looking as old as time but in fact a recent creation. (By rights it should surely only play different versions of Tristan and Iseult.) And then you come to the pale toboggan-steep sands of Porthcurno, with its eastern headland that looks as if it had been created by a

Opposite above:
The church at St Levan.

Opposite below:
Rosspletha Cross between Porthcurno and St Levan Church.

Overleaf:
The Marques rounding Pedn-mên-an-mere.

Left:
Nanjizal near Land's End.

Above:
Tater-du looking towards Boscawen Point.

The Logan Rock near Porthcurno.

Left:
Treryn Dinas, a pre-Celtic fort.

Above:
Sea mist over Pendeen.

Top:
Near Porthcurno.

flamboyant theatre designer to frame the cove. Near too is the Logan Rock, supposed to weigh eighty-four tons, and the Celtic – perhaps Druidic – fort of Treryn Dinas, with one of the finest of all views.

Even with this list one has overlooked Nanjizal, between Tol-Pedn-Penwith and Land's End, which in sunshine has an emerald sea and dazzling sands, and much further east Lamorna Cove at the foot of its bracken- and fern-grown valley, the walnut-brown cliffs giving depth and quality and irridescence to the sea they guard.

We spent the few days of our honeymoon at Mousehole – there being no petrol to venture further afield – and there saw the newly-imposed black-out for the first time. Walking out was a strange sensation. The fishing village, horse-shoed about its harbour, hummed like a disturbed hive. Not a light glimmered anywhere, and everyone had come out to see. Many of the villagers were sitting out on chairs in the soft September night; others sat on the sea wall; groups stood about arguing, gossiping. We had lost an aircraft carrier that

Opposite:
Granite rocks below the Logan Rock.

Below:
Mousehole. The village was used for the march of the rebellious miners in the first Poldark television series.

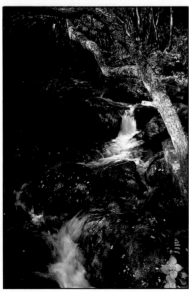

The contrasting landscapes near
Lamorna Cove range from barren
rocky coasts to misty wooded valleys.

Above:
Lamorna Cove. The fishing village
at Lamorna is typical of the
communities on the Penwith coast.
Sawle village in the *Poldark* novels is
a similar community.

Left:
A waterfall in the Lamorna valley
near the cove.

Right:
The Merry Maidens Stone Circle
near Lamorna.

Far right:
A wooded tributary of the Lamorna
valley.

day, torpedoed. Shipwreck and drowning were subjects with which most of the men and women in that village were all too familiar. An old fisherman came out of a pub and was hissed at for displaying a chink of light. 'Gor damme,' he complained, 'tes dark as a bloody sack.'

Our latest visit was last summer. Except for the NO PARKING signs and the double yellow lines, little in this area has changed. Although great efforts by various Chambers of Commerce have been made to promote an extension of the holiday season, the really intense congestion doesn't last much more than nine weeks. Anyway, there is a certain hazard about motoring round Mousehole at any time.

We stopped for a drink and sandwiches at the Lamorna Wink, an inn just at the approaches to Lamorna Cove. In the gentlemen's lavatory I heard two men talking. One said: 'Aw, I dearly love beer. I don't know whether 'tis more pleasurable takin' of it in or letten' of it out.'

The Cornish have a talent for aphorism.

★ ★ ★

Moorland road near St Ives.

*T*he north coast from St Ives to Land's End is also different from the rest of Cornwall. The narrow road which winds interminably among the stark grey hamlets has to negotiate shaggy boulders which lie everywhere hoary and hairy with time. The coaches and the cars may swarm and pullulate in the summer months on the car parks of Land's End, the sands of Whitesand Bay – never white – may turn black with cheerful holiday-makers; but they and their like – and we and our like – don't seem to put the essential land at risk: the massed palaeolithic rocks, if some old giant belched, could shake us all off in an afternoon. Drive in this area, as I have done more than once in the last few years, in an open car on a summer's night with the late dark just falling; or cross the old raised spine of land between St Ives and Penzance by way of Nancledra when a sea-mist is drifting in, and you will know what I mean.

There is much complaint about the ruination of Cornwall, and the complaints are hideously justifiable. (One thinks of Truro, to which I will come later.) But towns like Penzance and St Ives have on the whole preserved their identities in spite of economic pressures. The Penzance seafront – not the most picturesque – has not altered a jot in the long years I have known it; nor has the town except for a few one-way streets.

A mere village when it was burned by the Spaniards under Don Carlos de Amesquita who with his four prowling galleys landed there in July, 1595 – though it had graduated to the

A rainbow over St Ives.

Lanyon Quoit—a bronze age
chamber tomb, 1700–1500 BC.

status of a market town by the time Fairfax did the same thing to it half a century later – Penzance looks out over a mysterious bay, narrowly from Mousehole to Cudden Point, but more widely over the whole expanse of water from the Lizard to Tol-Pedn-Penwith. The bay was once a primeval forest: trees still project from the sand at low tide, and under the sand a black mould is what remains of leaf and branch and general vegetation. And possibly not so long ago – in geological time. The *Anglo-Saxon Chronicle* of 1014 records that 'in this year came that mickle sea flood, widely through this land, and it ran up so far as never at no time before; and it drowned many towns and mankind too innumerable to be computed.'

It is a paradox that this rather conventional-looking watering place should be the gateway to the most unquiet part of Cornwall and should preside over it all like a plump middle-aged nursemaid trying to look after a company of trolls. Everything about Penzance is reassuring: the anemones, the daffodils, the blue-green broccoli fields, the gentle slopes, the still water, the drowsing Mount, the verdant valleys. Nothing is less reassuring than the gaunt rock formations of Penwith just over the hill.

That other guardian of the Penwith peninsula on the north coast, St Ives, is almost literally another kettle of fish. Penzance genteelly devolves most of its fishing interests upon its rougher and more picturesque neighbour, Newlyn. St Ives carries on its fishing within the arms of its own harbour, and, until the ubiquitous tourist took over, this and mining were the trades by which its inhabitants lived and had their being: it has always been very matter-of-fact, down to earth in spite of its picturesque jumbled buildings and beautiful setting.

Nowadays it is quite difficult to get into the town: if you are a tourist you will be directed to a huge car park high above the town and will be expected to walk from there. It was the only solution short of a destruction of the town and the construction of giant car parks on the quays. Fortunately St Ives has set its face against any such thing; you can take it as it is or you don't take it at all.

Of course there has been much building, chiefly along the approach roads, most of it cheap and hideous, but the town itself has tried to keep its dignity and its individuality. There has been a recent scandal because the lifeboat house was retiled with red slates. The Council is insisting that they shall be taken off and replaced with grey. More honour to the Council. Sit on any of the beaches of St Ives and look back at the land. Note the colour and the elevations. Grey prevails everywhere, and low profiles. Compare this with the ravages of the French Riviera, of the Costa Brava, of Corfu.

Recently there has been a tragic loss of life when the Penlee lifeboat, near Mousehole on the other coast, was overturned while trying to rescue men from a shipwreck, and all the lifeboat crew was drowned. Few now perhaps will remember a similar disaster occurring to the St Ives lifeboat crew under Coxswain Cocking in 1938. I cannot remember whether there were any survivors from this crew – I think one – but I remember going down the following afternoon and looking at the lifeboat, the *John & Sarah Eliza Stych*, where it had been deposited by the sea upright on a flat reef of rock, almost undamaged-looking but empty of men. It was as if some great beast had swallowed them and spat out the husk. And the beast, still lashed by what was left of an eighty-mile-an-hour gale, provided a world of tumbling water and a mist of spume and spray drifting inwards across Trencrom Hill and wandering far overland towards the southern shore.

St Ives has a fine record for the courage of its lifeboat crews, and, before there were any lifeboats, the pilots, who seldom failed to risk their lives when ships in distress were blown into the bay. In the twenty-five years ending in 1848 over 150

vessels were wrecked on this coast between Cape Cornwall and Trevose, so there was opportunity enough for both heroism and acquisitiveness.

It is curious that it is the acquisitiveness which has entered into legends of the time. Of course wrecking was extensively practised. To a Cornishman a wreck was the spoils of the sea, just as surely as a shoal of fish. Wrecks were a gift of God, and few Wesleyans or other Christians were bothered by conscience in rushing down to the shore and seeing what the sea had brought them. High and low were equally involved. Indeed the lords of the various manors long claimed that any vessel or article from a vessel washed up on their foreshores was theirs by legal right. The pages of Cornish history are dotted with reports of claims and counter-claims, of conflicts on the beaches followed by conflicts in the courts, of stories of a mass of 'half-starved tynners' coming to a wreck with axes and picks and stripping it in a single tide. In 1764, when a French ship ran aground at Perranporth the entire cargo went in half a day and the crew were stripped to their shirts. A year or two later a Dutch vessel foundered at Porthleven laden with claret. In a day the miners cleared it all. Dr Borlase, writing in the middle of the eighteenth century, says: 'I have seen many a poor man, half dead, cast ashore and crawling out of reach of the waves, fallen upon and stripped naked by these villains, and if afterwards he had saved his chest or any clothes they have been taken from him.'

These were not isolated instances. It was of course a lawless age. But it is no more than two or three years since the residents of one of the south coast towns were prosecuted for stealing clocks, barometers and other things from a wreck and hiding them in their own houses. Nor were those prosecuted all Cornish.

But it is curious that this reputation attaches to the Cornish and not the other; for, apart from the great disasters when whole lifeboats are lost, such as the one at Penlee and the one at St Ives, which capture public sympathy and imagination, there have been far more cases of drowning men being saved from wrecks by the individual heroism of one or two men on the shore than there have ever been cases of carelessness being shown for their survival during the rush to grab the booty.

The other and more sinister meaning of wrecking – that is, the exhibition of false lights to lure a vessel on the rocks – seems to have been largely the invention of novelists who haven't bothered to read their history. You may turn the pages of the records back and back and you will find virtually nothing. It is true that the St Agnes light on the Scillies was something of a scandal for pretty well a hundred years after the tower was put up in 1680; you could never rely on how

Opposite above:
St Ives Bay from Godrevy Point.

Opposite below:
Whitesand Bay—Sennen Cove.

bright it was going to be or if it was going to be there at all. Eventually manning it was taken out of the hands of the Scillonians. And when Sir John Killigrew built the first lighthouse on the Lizard in 1619 the neighbouring villages complained bitterly that he was 'taking away God's grace from them'. He remarked that most of the houses in the district were built from ruined ships. But this is a long way from the lurid picture of villainous ruffians waving a lantern in the dark trying to lure the vessel ashore.

It was at St Ives – or next door Carbis Bay – where the BBC television crew and actors made their home during most of the shooting of the first sixteen episodes of *Poldark*. As a consequence many of the early scenes were taken in this general area. Mousehole was used for the scene of a miners' riot. Two houses – the back of one and the front of the other – were utilized for Nampara. One was Botallack Manor Farm, the other Pendeen Manor Farm, both near St Just in Penwith. Prussia Cove was taken for Nampara Cove. Porthcurno was used for the final scenes in Episode 16 where Ross and Demelza walk the beach together. Godolphin Hall near Breage was used for Trenwith.

Godolphin is another great name which has gone from Cornwall, leaving only a charming house behind. It was a Sir Francis Godolphin who led the motley forces he had hastily collected to resist the Spaniards when they landed at Mousehole and Penzance. In fact the servants and such as he led would have stood no chance against Spanish pikemen, but Don Carlos de Amesquita got wind of the approach of Drake and Hawkins from Plymouth and left in haste. Numbers of Sir Francis Godolphin's descendants or relatives became

Above:
A fishing fleet in Newlyn Harbour.

Above left:
A dawn scene at Mousehole.

Right:
Prussia Cove—used in the first
Poldark television series.

Overleaf
Cape Cornwall. A lane running
towards Priest's Cove lined with
fishermen's cottages.

governors of the Isles of Scilly, and a later Godolphin, one Sydney, was introduced at court as Groom of the Bed-chamber at the age of fifteen. Charles II said humorously of him that as a boy he was 'never in the way and never out of the way'. This attribute – and no doubt many others – served him well enough to enable him to become Lord High Treasurer to Queen Anne and the most successful prime minister of his time.

Script writers looking for a bit of melodrama at the end wrote into the last episode of the first series a scene in which miners went on the rampage and burned down Trenwith. This was staged at Godolphin Hall with the permission, but to the understandable consternation, of the present owner, Mr S. E. Schofield, who was concerned lest the semi-sham but over-realistic fires might melt the lead of his gutterings and down pipes.

When the second series was mounted it became necessary either to have builders apparently working on and repairing the fire-damaged Trenwith or to invent a new house. Since

Above:
Botallack Manor Farm—used as Nampara in the first Poldark television series.

Opposite:
A ruined mine chimney at St Just in Penwith.

The sand bar at Porthcurno, the scene of Demelza's solitary landing in a boat. The tidal currents made filming here too dangerous and an alternative location was found at Prussia Cove.

Aunt Agatha Poldark had not appeared in the first series – though she was very much in the books – it was decided to give her a house of her own to which George and Elizabeth could move, and this got over the problem of the gutted Trenwith. To portray this new house Boconnoc was chosen, much farther east in the county, near Lostwithiel.

All the great houses of Cornwall – to say nothing of many of the smaller ones – have a vivid history, and Boconnoc is no exception. At one time the property of the Earls of Devon – Sir Hugh Courtney, son and heir of the Earl, lived there in the mid-fifteenth century – it was sold in 1556 to the Mohun family, who continued in possession for over 160 years. Then in 1712, Charles, Lord Mohun became involved in a duel with the Duke of Hamilton, in which each shot the other dead, and Lady Mohun, his widow, having no issue, sold the whole estate of 8,000 acres to Thomas Pitt for £54,000. 'A cheap bargain,' it was remarked at the time.

Thomas Pitt, ex-governor of Madras, grandfather of the 1st Earl of Chatham and great-grandfather of the famous William, while in India had acquired from a Mr Jamchand,

who was one of the most eminent diamond merchants of his time, an enormous diamond for £20,400. It was said that Mr Jamchand first asked £85,000 for it and was gradually beaten down. Another bargain for Mr Pitt, for when he returned to England he had it cut in the form of a brilliant at a cost to him of £5,000, but immediately more than recouped the expense of this by selling the chips and filings. When finished the stone was round in shape, an inch broad, one and a sixth inches long, three-quarters of an inch thick, and weighed 136½ carats. Mr Pitt offered it to Queen Anne for £150,000. Queen Anne said she could not afford it. He then put it on the market and the stone was eventually bought by the Duke of Orléans, then Regent of France, for £135,000. He wore it in his hat, and later it was so worn by subsequent kings of France. It was stolen during the revolution and found again in a Paris garret, whereupon Napoleon pledged it to raise money to help him in his rise to power. At his coronation he had it fixed in the mouth of the gold crocodile that formed the pommel of his sword.

After his fall Marie Louise, his second wife, carried it away

Godolphin Hall—used as Trenwith in the first Poldark television series.

with her, but her father, the Emperor of Austria, returned it to France and it again became part of the French Crown jewels. Many of these were auctioned in 1887, but not The Regent, as it was now called, and when the Germans occupied Paris in 1940 it was sent to Chambord in the château country and hidden behind a stone panel. After the war it was once again returned to Paris, where it now is, on display in the Apollon Gallery of the Louvre.

In the meantime, however, Thomas Pitt, having paid £5,000 commission to an intermediary between himself and the Regent, had enough left over to buy a large estate in Hampshire and the delectable twelve and a half square miles of Boconnoc. It has never been on the market since.

Because of a family dispute the furniture of the big house was left away from the inheritor of the estate, so the present owner, faced with the impossible expense of entirely refurnishing it, now lives in a handsome dower house nearby, and the great house stands empty, a prey to wind and weather. It made a most handsome house for Aunt Agatha (who in the novels hasn't a bean) and lit up superbly for a number of great occasions.

★ ★ ★

In the thirties, when I first saw Cornwall, and no doubt for generations before, there was in process a constant brain-drain from the county. A boy who was clever at school went up-country to work, usually coming back to his native county only for holidays or for retirement. He had no choice: there were no opportunities for him in Cornwall. Boys whose parents could afford to send them to a university or those who by their own unaided efforts got scholarships to a university – an infinitely difficult task because of the sheer lack of value of the few scholarships that could be won – such boys scarcely came back at all. This meant that – at least academically – Cornwall was constantly deprived of its brightest young men. It was a backwater with a wonderful history and not much present.

Then, after World War II, what had been in the between-war years a trickle of up-country people seeking retirement or a more distant view of the rat-race, became a flood. Improved roads and improved motor cars made this possible. The Great Western Railway had coined – or had made the most of – the phrase 'The Cornish Riviera'. It is largely nonsense but it has worked. An eighteenth-century writer describing the weather in Cornwall said that 'the winters are like March and the summers like April.' This is nearer the truth; yet hundreds – indeed, thousands – have found the strange, fickle, exhilarating climate to their liking and settled in the county. In many districts Cornish people have been almost submerged. Today it is a delight to go to Gloucestershire and hear the authentic accent spoken by nine out of ten people you meet. In Cornwall if you speak to a stranger the chances are about three to one that his accent will be north country or midland. Fortunately there are still substantial areas – strong pockets – resistant to infiltration and change, but the overall picture is depressingly of a native population overwhelmed by 'immigration'.

Let us not, of course, deceive ourselves. Since the collapse of the mining and fishing industries, the economy of Cornwall has come to depend on the 'foreigner'. It is not much good dubbing him an 'emmet' if you rely on him for nine-tenths of whatever prosperity you can muster. I personally deplore the gimcrack bungalows and chalets, the unsightly and badly sited caravan parks, the exploitation of many of the lovely beaches and coves, the flood of visitors who swirl down the various motorways – crowding the beaches, sleeping by the roadside, overstraining the medical resources, even the funeral facilities, making life almost impossible for the natives and almost impossible for themselves.

There is no answer – except the perfectionist one, and one not practical of attainment: that of spreading the same number of visitors over twenty weeks instead of ten; or the disagreeable answer of the last two summers, when the depression has thinned out the numbers and it has been possible to live in Cornwall in a degree of comfort even in August.

Anyway, apart from economic setbacks the process is irreversible. The bungalows, the chalets, the exploitations have come to stay. Oddly enough, the residents I find most bitter about the annual flood of holiday-makers are usually non-Cornish who have been settled in the county only a few years themselves.

And of course the substantial core of the Cornish remain. And it is a very hard core. A writer stated a few years ago: 'By the frequent peregrination of the natives and the continual ingress of strangers, those local habits which might once have been deemed unconquerable have almost completely disappeared.'

This is from John Heard's *A Survey of the County of Cornwall*, 1817. So perhaps there is hope yet.

★　★　★

Above:
A farmhouse in the hamlet of
Demelza.

Above right:
The present-day owners of the farm.
The family of these brothers has
been here for over two hundred
years.

When my parents moved to Cornwall I was, as I have already indicated, greatly taken with the scene. But I understood nothing about the Cornish. They were a closed Celtic book whose pages did not open easily to the outsider, the importation. It was a mutual barrier. There is – or was in those days, and I don't think it has altogether gone – a tinge of superiority felt by people holidaying or just making their homes in the county for the first time. Coming from other parts of England, they feel themselves more sophisticated, more up-to-date. However inexcusable that was – and is – it was and is detectable in conversation, in behaviour, in attitudes. The words of the Cornish Floral Dance are as good an illustration as any. 'That quaint old Cornish Town.' It's so damned patronizing. There is nothing fundamentally more quaint about Helston than there is, say, about Honiton, and not as much as about Hastings, which is an extraordinary place. It is a pseudo-romantic, pixies-and-elves approach, of which as a youth I was probably as guilty as the rest, and it took some years for me to throw off this ridiculous attitude and to get to know the Cornish. I do not think I made any special effort to do this. Perhaps it was more successful because it came naturally – by little and by little. Living among them I came to know them, understand them a bit, and to like them. I think they liked me. A certain empathy developed.

My early novels – and Heaven help me, they were all published – were modern thrillers, and except for one Cornish one – which like most of the others I have mercifully been able to suppress – were set in other parts of the country: London, Yorkshire, Wales, the Wye Valley, etc.

Above:
A lobster fisherman off the Penwith peninsula.

Opposite:
A Kellynack farmer leaning on an ancient granite post.

Overleaf:
Demelza's Cove, near Seal Hole Cave. The scene of Demelza's meeting with Hugh Armitage.

By the time *Poldark* came to be written, it was not only the scenery of Cornwall that had got into my blood. I had never written a historical novel before – that is, if one excepts *The Forgotten Story*, a novel of Cornwall in 1898 (of which a television serial has recently been made).

Perhaps inevitably to begin with *Poldark* was derivative; but presently it took off on tracks of its own and I think has been pursuing them ever since. I certainly had no idea then when or how far the tracks would lead. It was to be one novel. But the stream broadened so much in the writing that there was no way of containing it in a single volume. The story of Ross and Demelza and George and Elizabeth could have been so contained: indeed, if pressed, one could write the elements of their story on a postcard. But as I wrote about them what happened to them came to be part of the warp and woof of eighteenth-century life, in which Jud and Prudie Paynter, Jim and Jenny Carter, Mark and Keren Daniel and a half dozen others emerged to claim a substantial share. And this has gone on, more characters emerging as others have faded out.

Quimper are chiefly taken from accounts given by Lady Ann Fitzroy who for a time was imprisoned there.

The struggle for power in Truro and the quarrel between Lord Falmouth and the Burgesses supported by Sir Francis Basset. It almost all derived from the contents of a single letter written by Mr Henry Rosewarne, the MP newly elected in defiance of the Boscawen interest, addressed to Lord Falmouth, explaining the reasons for the Corporation's defiance and defending his own actions. Corroborative information came of course from Cornelius Cardew and others.

The riots in Camborne, Sir Francis Basset's suppression of them, the death penalty for three of the rioters, two reprieved, one, Peter Hoskin, hanged: all factual.

The character of Monk Adderley was based on a character in the original William Hickey Diaries. Details of the duel between Adderley and Ross came largely from the life of John Wilkes.

The run on Pascoe's Bank in Truro, the pressure by the other banks, the anonymous letters deliberately circulated to create a panic. All factual, except not exactly as to date.

Dwight Enys saving the injured miner by giving him what is now called 'the kiss of life'. From a case related in John Knyveton's *Surgeon's Mate*.

So in the case of the Penzance lifeboat.

So in the case of the stage-coach.

And so on in many smaller details.

★   ★   ★

*O*f course there is the opposite risk, that of becoming too preoccupied with history. One can so easily detect the midnight oil, the desire to instruct. But novels are about life. Text books by the thousand exist if a reader wishes to pursue a particular subject. An author is naturally reluctant, once he has discovered something at great trouble to himself, not to make the most of it. But the temptation should be resisted. It is a recurring discipline which should be exercised by every novelist who does research, whether the research is into the Peninsular War or into modern techniques of assassination. What is not relevant is irrelevant.

Launceston Gaol.

Above:
Tresungers Bay.

Opposite:
A small cove from the two hundred-foot-high cliffs on Kelsey Head
near Porth Joke.

The Poldark World

*A*nyway, for better or for worse, the Poldark world is one I have myself inhabited over long periods of my life, with a personal sense of benefit from the absorption. The first four novels were written between 1945 and 1953 and were interspersed with two of the new suspense novels which were to lead me away from Cornwall (as to subject) in the next few years. Indeed in the succeeding two decades I wrote only one historical novel, *The Grove of Eagles*, which was about sixteenth-century Cornwall, and eight modern novels. Although these were infinitely more successful, the Poldark novels never went out of print, and a steady trickle of letters came all through these years asking me to continue them.

*T*here didn't seem much prospect. I had drifted away to a different style and pattern. My work had become more sophisticated, less romantic. I was older. The mood had passed. Also, although the suspense novels of the fifties had been successful – three made into films, another bought but not made, bookclub choices in America, translations – those of the sixties were more so, with Hitchcock making *Marnie* into a film, MGM making *The Walking Stick*, Paramount (at one remove) buying *Angell, Pearl and Little God* and several companies taking out abortive options on the only other novel of that period, *After the Act*. There was absolutely no inducement for me to change direction, no purpose in going back.

It would take too long to analyse the creative stirrings and conflicts which decided the change of course. Paradoxically it may have been my *absence* from Cornwall at that time which was one of the factors conducive to the return to the Poldarks.

One never knows in what devious ways nostalgia may work. I can only short-circuit it all by saying that in 1971 it became creatively stimulating to consider a return.

From the consideration to the act was infinitely difficult. Whereas I have always moved easily, indeed with a sense of refreshment and challenge, from one style to the other, from the tauter, compact modern novels, to the more leisurely, broader-canvassed historical stories, it was not so here; for I was not just reverting to another style, I was reverting to books already written long ago, picking up characters and situations, assuming and reconciling attitudes and differences, putting on clothes which – possibly – I had outgrown. I didn't dare to read the first four books through, for I knew if I did that that would finish it. Not necessarily from a critical point of view; but if you want an appetite for a subject you don't eat a big meal first. Only sufficient dippings to refresh the memory. And I found to my surprise how much had been remembered: it was as if the characters had remained dormant in the subconscious waiting for the word.

Even so for the first hundred pages it was like breaking the sound barrier. Then everything began to move more steadily, more easily and as if predestined to a particular end.

Since then, apart from a book of short stories, a history of the Anglo-Spanish war of the sixteenth century, and two re-written earlier novels, it has been all Poldark. It is interesting to reflect that when I began *The Black Moon* – the first of the new Poldarks – I went to see my accountant and warned him that I was turning to my 'non-profit making activities'. Thanks to television, it hasn't turned out that way.

Above:
Trevellas Porth with St Agnes in the background.

Above left:
The Bawden Rocks, or Man and his man, from Trevellas Porth.

Left:
The harbour at Port Isaac – used in the first series of *Poldark*.

Page 158:
Overlooking the harbour at Port Isaac.

Page 159:
Cottages at Port Isaac.

Pages 160–61:
Port Quin viewed from the coast with Roscarrock on the skyline.

There had in fact been an earlier attempt to make the first four novels into a film. In 1969 Associated British Pictures bought an option and commissioned a producer and a writer to prepare the ground for a big film. It was intended to last about four hours and be a sort of Cornish *Gone with the Wind*. On the 11th March of that year in torrential rain I drove down with my wife to meet the producer, Kenneth Harper, and the writer, Vincent Tilsley, at the Carlyon Bay Hotel at St Austell. We spent five days in Cornwall with them, moving to the Greenbank Hotel, Falmouth on the 13th. The weather was horrible, drizzle and mist every day, but we saw many of the scenes that the film was intended to show.

I took them to Port Isaac and Roscarrock and Port Quin and to Trevellas Porth. At Trevellas the mist was thick and ghostly. We had slithered our way down in two big cars almost to the edge of the sea. It was not a pretty road, having been used for more than twenty years for test trials on the London to Land's End motor rally: hairpin bends and surfaces of loose stone and rock. The old mineshafts loomed in the mist, the sea muttered on the rocks, a solitary gull told us of its bereavement. Vincent said he would like to go off on his own for a bit. He was obviously inspired, and we waited for him there in the damp, clammy mist, not speaking ourselves, listening perhaps for the tramp of long-dead miners, for the hiss and suck of the long-silent engines, for the clang of the long-fallen changing bell. Nothing had altered here except time and weather, turning it all to rubble and to waste.

The following day we went to St Day, the very centre of the old copper mining belt, to Redruth and Camborne, stopped at South Crofty, where a mine still worked and was in profit, then to St Ives and Penzance. In the few days we saw much, and then we all returned to London.

Vincent Tilsley wrote a very good script, but inevitably the story had to be hideously slashed. And even more would have had to come out, for his script as written would have run for at least five fours.

However I need not have been concerned. (If concerned is the word.) Unknown to us, a financial battle was developing in London with EMI trying to take over Associated British Pictures. After months of conflict they won, and, it being the invariable custom of incoming moguls to axe any projects initiated by outgoing moguls, *Poldark* was axed. It was five years after this, when I was writing *The Four Swans*, that London Films, having bought an option on the television rights, eventually interested the BBC in a joint production.

Between the two events there was a connection in that Mr Robert Clark, chairman of ABP at the time of the take-over and the force behind the proposed Poldark production, later became chairman of London Films and again activated this interest. London Films is the old Alexander Korda company and continued its existence to market the many Korda films which are still in demand throughout the world. Its collaboration with the BBC over *Poldark* was the first of its kind, and was later followed by *I Claudius*, *Thérèse Raquin* and *Testament of Youth*.

So early in 1975 it all began.

★ ★ ★

On the north coast of Cornwall, not far from Padstow but separated from it by the River Camel and by the parish of St Minver, is the parish of St Endellion. According to William Hals, the name comes from a Saint Delian, a British saint, who died about the year 570, though the church itself is dedicated to a later saint person called Endelienta. The square tower of this fine church is clearly visible from a long way out at sea and for centuries has been used as a landmark by coasting vessels. The parish has three natural inlets: Port Isaac, Port Gaverne and Port Quin.

The first and best known of these is still largely unspoiled because it lies like a cramped grey fist at the bottom of precipitous hills, with lanes narrow enough to intimidate all but the hardiest motorist. John Betjeman perceptively calls it 'a steep sunless place, free from storms'. It is a charming little port, the tiny cottages of slate and granite nudging each other down the hill to the quay, square yards of garden blossoming here and there, a stream trickling and bubbling from one ledge to another till it reaches the harbour wall and runs out upon the beach.

Sunless? A strange description. I have always seen it in brilliant sunlight.

Yet the same adjective applies to the third inlet of Port Quin – and with more reason; or more psychological reason. Once a thriving fishing village, it is now totally derelict, and preserved from reanimators of the wrong sort by the National Trust. John Norden, the Elizabethan topographer, describes it as being 'all decayed since the growing up of Port Isaac', yet its ruined fish cellars speak of a much more recent prosperity – or at least activity. In the middle of the last century it was still exporting slate and importing coal. There are also old lead and antimony mines near by.

The story is told that all the men of the village were drowned at sea in the fishing boat they jointly owned, and that afterwards their widows and children drifted away leaving the cottages to become derelict. It is a story which exactly fits the

brooding scene, and one feels that if it isn't true it ought to be. In fact there seems to be no historical basis for it; but my own feeling is that so strong a folk memory as this cannot altogether be disregarded. I would guess that, in the nineteenth century and before, there were fishing fatalities in the village – with such a coast it is unlikely there would not be – and that these bore more heavily on a tiny community than they would on a larger one; that the sad widows moved away, their children finding more profitable work elsewhere, that its need as a fishing port died with the failure of the pilchard shoals, that Port Isaac catered better for the slate and the coal, that cottages became empty because no one wanted them, that the deaths and drownings which had occurred off and on through the years slowly merged in the collective mind into the tragedy of a single night.

This inlet was used extensively by the BBC both in the first Poldark series and the second. In the second it was completely transformed in the course of two days into Sawle village, with fishing boats of the period, stalls, baskets, nets, brooms,

Above:
A fisherman wheeling lobster pots at Penberth Cove.

Opposite:
The Camel estuary at Daymer Bay.

Above:
Padstow and the River Camel from Brae Hill near Daymer Bay.

Left:
The River Camel.

trivets, trestles, pots and pans, and dozens of extras, old women sewing in doorways, fishermen carrying lobster pots, little girls in mob caps, dogs and donkeys, and chickens picking among the cobbles.

In the first series it was the locale chosen for the famous wrecking episode, when hungry drunken miners spill upon the beach and fight over the brandy and the silks and the provisions being washed inshore from the wreck. This was a tremendously difficult scene to render realistically and involved the use again of dozens of extras, recruited locally as in all these big scenes. The best account of the filming of this scene is to be found in Robin Ellis's booklet, *Making Poldark*.

Nearby is the Gothic folly, built like a miniature castle on Doyden Point, which was used for the Gatehouse in the novels, where Dwight Enys lived and illegally loved Keren Daniel. And nearby too, of course, is Roscarrock, which to me has always been partly Nampara, even though it sits in a shallow fold of land overlooking the sea and not at the foot of a valley.

The manor of Roscarrock was held at the time of Edward the Confessor by one, Alwin; at the time of the Domesday Book by Nigel: a change, possibly, to Norman ownership. A first recorded Richard de Roscarrock died there in 1300. His son married into the Arundells (almost inevitably it seems), and *his* son became a member of parliament for the county in 1347 and 8 – just after Crécy and just before the Black Death. We do not know if he died of it, but his family continued to prosper in their handsome castellated manor house and son-to-son inherited for 370 years.

Early in the sixteenth century John married Agnes Grenville of Stowe, a union which linked the Roscarrocks with another powerful county family but one which was to become fiercely Protestant in the years ahead. When it came to the crunch, however, most of the grandchildren of this union were loyal to the old faith and suffered for it. One at least was racked, and three-quarters of the Roscarrock possessions were for a time sequestered to the Queen.

But the family continued in possession until about 1880 (though the 'great estate by ill conduct, was much wasted') when the last Roscarrock sold what was left to Edward Boscawen of Tregothnan. Thereafter it passed through many hands and was largely pulled down and rebuilt as a farm house, though some of the old part remains: a chapel-like ruin, an oriel window, a fine arched timber roof, and a ghost.

It was here that the Poldarks almost made themselves a home. Apart from its alias as Nampara, the outbuildings were used for Sawle Feast, for the capture of Ned Hoskin and for a number of other unrelated scenes. It is so completely

Opposite above:
View from Roscarrock. Ross used to ride across the hilltops in the background.

Opposite below:
The grain barn at Roscarrock — where Jud Paynter ran when the dog bit him. The granite supports of the barn were designed to keep rats out.

Roscarrock—scene of the hanging of
Ned Hoskin.

Left:
St Enodoc Church. Used for the wedding of
Rowella Chynoweth and Arthur Solway.

Above:
Doyden Point near Port Quin, used in the first series
of *Poldark* as Dwight Enys' house, where Keren
Daniel came visiting.

undisturbed, with winding lanes, largely unsignposted, and cart tracks leading to the farm.

I remember the day in early 1977 when I first took the producer of the second series and the production manager to see the farm. Conditions could hardly have been worse. We had been inspecting a number of locations, and the day, gloomy and damp to begin, had blown up to a force 7 wind, and 'misty-wet' was moving over the land. Car doors flung open or slammed, ruts were filling with water and turning into mud, screenwipers were wheezing, every movement out of the cars meant a dash with dripping face to some sort of shelter. We arrived eventually in the cobbled yard outside the front door – where Ross and Demelza were to greet each other so often –, and the two BBC men drove further on to look at the stables. As I turned my own car round and settled to wait for them the front door opened and the lady of the house put her head out. 'Have you lost your way, dear?' she said benignly to my wife. 'Would you like to come in and have a cup of tea?'

We accepted – and it was one of many over the succeeding months – often with the offer of a little something added 'to keep the cold out'.

The production manager had seen the property before when prospecting for the first series; but the owners would not agree to the use of the farm. It was only after observing the exemplary behaviour of the BBC unit when filming at Port Quin in the first series that they changed their minds. It took the new producer only ten minutes to make up *his* mind that wet day that he wanted to use it. 'This has got everything,' he said.

Not far from here – though actually in the parish of St Minver – is the ancient church of St Enodoc, where Arthur Solway (in the series) married Rowella Chynoweth. It is mainly thirteenth century, and not so long ago was half covered in blown sand. When Bishop Phillpotts visited it in 1851 he had to climb in through the roof, the sands having blown higher than the eastern gable, the pews being worm eaten, and bats living in the roof and belfry. Fourteen years later it was restored and a good wall built round the churchyard to keep out further encroachments. Today it looks pretty safe, being separated from the dunes by a field and part of a golf course. Its little blunt mediaeval spire sticks up out of its protective belt of tamarisk trees like the snout of an ant-eater waking from a doze.

Filming the French sequences presented an obvious problem of logistics. (These were the sequences in which Dwight Enys is rescued from a prisoner-of-war camp.) For a while it was expected that we should go over to Quimper in

Opposite:
The interior of St Enodoc Church.

Above:
King Harry Ferry.

Above right:
The ferry with laid-up oil tankers.

Brittany and film the sequences on the spot; but this proved too expensive an operation and it was decided that for these scenes parts of Cornwall must be turned into France. A long search for the prison camp included the inspection of several castellated houses and sites, from the relatively modern Caerhays to the Norman Restormel; but eventually St Mawes Castle was picked on and renamed for the purpose Fort Baton.

Henry VIII, fearing an attack on England by Francis I of France, decided to build a succession of castles along the English coast to defend it. The legend is that he came down to Cornwall with his ministers, and with Anne Boleyn, and that to demonstrate his prowess to her he swam his horse across the River Fal at a place which has ever since been called King Harry's Passage or King Harry Ferry. Again, as far as I know, there is no evidence for any of this. In any event, if he was on terms of happy friendship with Anne, the date can hardly have been later than about 1530, and St Mawes Castle was not begun until ten years later. This of course proves or disproves nothing. St Mawes Castle now squats on its elegant promontory looking across at Pendennis Castle, Falmouth, which was built – or entirely rebuilt – under the same edict and at the same time.

Between them they dominate the wide blue expanse of the River Fal; which at its mouth is perhaps the finest natural harbour in England and one of the half dozen best in the world. The Fal used to be navigable as far as Tregony; over the centuries it has so silted up that it now only just reaches Truro, though on full moons it sweeps up across the shallow muddy bird-haunted reaches and turns Truro into the port it

View from Trelissick House towards the River Fal.

once used to be. Even so the water is so deep at King Harry Ferry that vessels of 10,000–15,000 tons are moored there – in moth-balls until the shipping depression passes.

One of the tributaries of the River Fowey, the River Lerryn, near Tregays, was used for the River Odet in France. This area is so blissfully uninhabited that a platoon of French soldiers marching through the woods and sharp exchanges of musket fire across the river hardly had to be explained to anyone.

★ ★ ★

Filmed in 1975 and 1977, *Poldark* missed the perfect summer of 1976. 1975 was also exceptionally good, 1977 more predictably unreliable.

Porthluney Beach was to be used in May '77. This is the beach overlooked by the magnificent Nash-designed Caerhays Castle, built by a Trevanion who bankrupted himself in the process, but which has been in the hands of the Williams family since 1852. A succession of the Williamses have been

Caerhays Castle.

garden lovers of a special kind, and John Charles Williams financed expeditions to the Himalayas to bring back rare camellias and rhododendrons. One can think of few more delightful or civilized ways of spending money. The Williamsii Camellia, first grown at Caerhays, is one of the most valuable hybrid shrubs ever produced, and now has an extensive progeny. Hilliers of Winchester alone name twenty-four of them.

The great gardens of south Cornwall in April and May are a rare sight. Where there are perhaps ten such show-pieces it is invidious to pick one out; but Caerhays must be considered pre-eminent, with perhaps Penjerrick second.

(Sussex, surprisingly, considering its sharper, dryer climate, is also renowned for its fine rhododendron and azalea gardens. When I bought a house in Sussex I first made sure that the soil was suitable for rhododendrons. Of course the ideal thing for a rhododendron lover is to have had a grandfather who planted them; but it's surprising all the same what one can do in a relatively few years.)

★   ★   ★

Porthluney where Ross galloped across the beach when returning to Nampara at the beginning of the second television series.

*P*orthluney Beach, then, below Caerhays, May '77. The beach was to be used for two scenes: one when Ross (the splendid Robin Ellis) is returning from the wars and gallops across the beach from one side to the other, his black cloak flowing in the wind. The other was for when Morwenna and her young charge Geoffrey Charles are playing on the beach, and Drake Carne comes across and speaks to them and they go to the Holy Well together.

The day was foul: a force 6–7 wind with showers of tropical violence – in distinctly sub-tropical temperatures. Everybody was cold and wet and miserable. The weather for the first shot did not so much matter: nobody dictated what sort of a day it was when Ross returned. But when Morwenna and Geoffrey Charles and Drake are on the beach it is supposed to be fine and sunny; they paddle and run about enjoying themselves in the sun. Cameras can perform miracles these days, persuading the viewer it is a nice day when in fact it is a nasty one. (Instance soccer and rugby matches played in constant rain which appear clear and bright on the television screen.) But actors can't actually *act* that sort of a scene in torrential rain, so it became a question of dodging the showers, crouching under umbrellas and suddenly emerging dry and smiling for a five-minute rehearsal or a two-minute take before the next flood of rain blew up. Technicians covered their cameras and crouched under capes, cold rain dripping round their feet.

Opposite:
Porthluney Beach.

I passed one of them just emerging like a tortoise from under his mackintosh. 'Awful day!' I said.

'Oh, I don't mind it,' he replied, wiping rain off his face. 'I don't mind it at all. Thing is, I'm alive, I'm well, and I'm working.'

It's a great philosophy. Would that we all had it.

Portholland Beach near to Porthluney was chosen to be Roscoff in Brittany. This is a tiny rock-ribbed inlet with a few boat houses and fish sheds which were quickly transformed into a corner of a French fishing port. Surprisingly a corrugated iron roof escaped the scrutiny of the scene setter – and no viewer seems to have complained.

Tehidy, the home of Sir Francis Basset, was burned down in 1919, and only a few ruins and a part of the orangery remain. Shortly afterwards it was rebuilt as a sanatorium. So Lanhydrock – another National Trust property – near Bodmin was used in the film in its place.

About the beginning of the sixteenth century a young man from Truro called Richard Roberts, of lowly birth, married Anne Jeffery from Breage and with the small money that she brought him began to trade in timber. By her he had two sons and five daughters, and his business prospered to the extent of his becoming a rich man. When he died he left his eldest son,

Portholland used as Roscoff in the television series.

also Richard, with enough money to put out considerable sums to usury, and his debtors paid him in tin. He, 'engrossing the sale of tin', came to be worth many thousands, also his brother John, whose son became Baron Truro. The family changed its name from Roberts to Robartes, and by 1620 was able to buy land and property once belonging to the old priory of Bodmin, a beautiful site at the head of the valley running down to the River Fowey. There, at Lanhydrock, they built the finest Jacobean house in Cornwall, and from James I bought a barony which remained in being until the last Robartes, Viscount Clifden, died in 1966.

Like Tehidy, Lanhydrock suffered from a disastrous fire – this in 1881 – but the Robartes family – or Agar-Robartes by then – were still sufficiently prosperous to rebuild it much as it had been before, so that superficially it is still a splendid Jacobean mansion, and, except for the greater amenities for comfortable living, no one would ever know. It has one of the finest approaches a house could have, laid about with lawns and trees and flowering shrubs; it has a handsome picture gallery and the most perfectly situated billiards room I have

ever seen. (Although I visited it once when it was still a private house, I did not play. It seems a pity.)

This time, 1977, while filming was taking place in the gardens, I paid it another private visit, this to call on Miss Foy Quiller-Couch, who had a small flat in the house. Although a lady then in her mid-seventies, she came skimming down three flights of stairs to greet me, and as airily re-climbed them. For me it was a brief pilgrimage of friendship and respect for her father, whom I had never met but many of whose books I have greatly admired. We sat sipping sherry under Sir Arthur's portrait. Miss Quiller-Couch told me how disappointed she was that none of her father's books was in print and there was no prospect of a reissue. I offered to have a shot myself, and when I returned to London made an effort to persuade the publishers I knew, but without result. However I gather some have now been republished.

I mentioned to Foy Quiller-Couch that we had recently been filming a wedding scene at St Winnow on the River Fowey, and she said: 'When I was young my father used to row my mother and me from our home up to Sunday morning

Above:
An avenue of beeches at Lanhydrock.

Overleaf:
Lanydrock used in the second BBC series as Sir Francis Basset's house. Originally Jacobean, Lanhydrock was rebuilt in the mid-nineteenth century and is now owned by the National Trust.

Above:
Detail of a Cornish Perpendicular
window at St Winnow Church.

Right:
St Winnow Church—used in the
second BBC television series for the
wedding of Dwight Enys and
Caroline Penvenen. The River Fowey
is in the background.

service at St Winnow and back to Fowey when it was over.' The words brought up a deeply nostalgic picture of a time now altogether gone, of Sir Arthur, probably in a straw hat and in shirt sleeves with a black silk waistcoat, rowing the two ladies five miles with the incoming tide; they with light frocks and pretty hats and parasols, of them stepping ashore at the tiny quay, assuming a greater air of sobriety as their man assumed his coat and they went in to church; and, if the parson's sermon was long-winded, of Sir Arthur taking out his watch and looking at it surreptitiously lest the tide should ebb too far and leave them stranded.

The wedding of Dwight Enys and Caroline Penvenen at St Winnow was one of the highlights of the second series, for everyone had to be there, almost all the main members of the cast, in gay wedding attire. Fortunately for those scenes the weather was splendid. It was a joyous three days.

The principle on which these series were made was that, while the producer remained constant, a different writer and a different director should do each book. I'm not sure what special ends this arrangement served, except those of speed; but I was lucky in each series in what I might call my middle directors: Kenneth Ives who directed *Jeremy Poldark* and Roger Jenkins who directed *The Four Swans*. Roger Jenkins, whose methods of direction were not the most organized, yet had some artistic quality which gave his four episodes a different depth and excellence: you never realized it until you saw it on the screen.

For the wedding scene, when the married couple drove away in a handsome coach, followed by the good wishes, the hand-wavings and the happy smiles of the guests (a lovely picture with the background of the church and the river with its massed banks of trees) Roger felt he needed a foreground incident to give the scene a greater truth to the time. As the coach moved away over the rough lane a girl should be seen milking a cow nearby and the cow should be startled by the passing of the coach. The cow was no problem, but where was the milkmaid? East Cornwall was scoured. Everything was mechanical. No one it appeared knew even *how* to milk a cow. Eventually a milkmaid was found: she was seventy-three . . .

★ ★ ★

Quin Cottage, Port Quin—used in the first BBC television series as Captain Blamey's house.

People often ask where I found the names used in these novels. Poldark – unlike most of them – is a pure invention. When I was in my early twenties my best friend was a young chemist called Ridley Polgreen. He was some years older than I was, and died tragically when he was thirty-two. He was not remotely like Ross Poldark, being a strict

Wesleyan, non-smoking, non-drinking, but with a tremendously lively sense of humour and a deep appreciation of all that was good and beautiful in life. When I wished to choose a name, I thought first to use the name Polgreen. Then it seemed to me better that I should use a name no one else had ever had; also Polgreen seemed not quite strong enough. So the name Poldark came into being.

Since those days many people have used the name Poldark – usually without asking my permission – to cash in on the extra publicity created by the television series.

The physical appearance of Ross Poldark comes from a chance acquaintance I made in a railway train just after World War II. A young flying officer was sitting facing me. He was tall, lean, bony, scarred, withdrawn but pleasant, heavy lids over eyes of that pale blue that doesn't flinch at much. He was, he said, convalescing after a crash: broken leg, couple of ribs, scratch on his face; lucky really. Just waiting to pass his fitness test; any day now. A quiet man but tense, purposeful. A vein in his neck; a sort of high-strung disquiet. I took in everything I could about him, knowing, knowing this was to be the man.

Just after I had chosen the name for the main character and for the family, I was driving across the Goss Moor between Roche and Bodmin, and saw a signpost. It read Demelza. For many months I had had the female character somewhat vaguely in my mind, a dark haired waif whom Ross picked up at Redruth Fair, but I could find no name and no proper identity for her. The signpost changed all that. Not only did it provide the name; by that curious alchemy which sometimes happens to writers, the character became vivid at the same time. To me, at least, it has never faded.

So Demelza became a girl's Christian name. The first girl to be so named in real life was Demelza Val Baker, the daughter of Denys Val Baker, the novelist and essayist. She must by now be well over thirty, but there have been many more since.

Years later, having passed the signpost many times, for it is just off the A30 London road, I went to see this village whose name had been such an inspiration. It proved to be no more than a hamlet with a single Chapel (once United Methodist Free Church but now all part of the greater body) and two small farms, one of which had been in the same family, son to son, since the seventeenth century.

What does the name mean? According to Dr William Pryce, author of *Mineralogia Cornubiensis*, that definitive book on eighteenth-century mining, writing in his other book, *An Essay to Preserve the Ancient Cornish Language*, published in 1790, *De* means the or thy, and *Melza* means

Above:
The road to Warleggan.

Left:
The Church of St Bartholomew, Warleggan.

Above:
A moorland wall near Warleggan.

Above right:
The Methodist chapel at Bosullow
Common on West Penwith Moor.

honey or sweetness (links here, presumably, with the French *miel*). It's a nice thought; and I hope it is not too far out to consider the name means 'Thy sweetness'.

Nampara, incidentally, means 'The Valley of Bread'. It is an extraordinary coincidence that this tiny district of Perranporth, before the Great Western Railway built its line there and effaced local landmarks, was renowned for its bakery. Yet the name goes back centuries. Coincidence? Or is it just conceivable, considering the unchanging nature of the English – and Cornish – countryside, that the name did not pre-date the nature of the occupation carried on there?

Warleggan was another name taken from a village – this one on the Bodmin moors. A lonely place, and one it is almost impossible to get to without traversing the desolate moorland. Unaltered for centuries, the narrow roads squeeze and twist between blocks of moorstone piled to make the hedge walls, with cattle grids to cross and ancient ramshackle wooden gates green with lichen. The last time I was there was in mid-June. A cold south-easterly wind was blowing wet fog over everything, and I would not have fancied straying more than twenty yards from any beaten track. The village is down a steep hill – just straying off the moor – the church squat and low, built of the same moorland granite, with a grey short tower – relic of a spire struck by lightning – a few unkempt and ancient tombstones, a plain altar, an organ boxed with wood, wild anchusa flowering beside the steps as you go in. But follow the hill further down and you come upon one of the paradoxes peculiar to Cornwall: a harsh, wind-scoured countryside cleft suddenly by a valley, which in this case contains the River Warleggan, a bubbling sylvan stream overhung with elms and lush beeches and lined with cow parsley and hart's tongue ferns. From one vegetation to the other is not a mile.

It is perhaps not inappropriate that this gaunt lonely little village should give its name to the family in the books – a family based on two other such which in fact flourished in the eighteenth and nineteenth centuries in Cornwall.

The church of St Bartholomew, Warleggan, is one which has had a reputation for eccentric parsons. One, it is said, used to cut out figures in cardboard and prop them up to fill his church with his missing parishioners. Another – or perhaps it was the same – wrote in the service book: 'No fog, no wind, no rain, no drizzle, no congregation.' Perhaps the moors breed eccentricity. Some forty years ago a church not far from Warleggan was visited by the rural dean, Mr Edward Tilson-Morgan, who was shocked by the condition of the fabric, and said so. The vicar smiled eagerly and replied: 'Ah, yes, quite so, my dear sir, I quite agree. But have you seen my mouse-traps?'

Tregirls is another hamlet on the Bodmin moors, just south of Altarnun. This worked the opposite way round. The name lodged in my memory and fretted and intrigued until a character grew out of it: the one-armed asthmatic rascal Tholly Tregirls.

Clowance, Ross's daughter, was the name of the family home of the St Aubyns for centuries and is in the parish of Crowan. Cuby is a small parish near Tregony on the River Fal.

Opposite above:
Woodland near Boconnoc.

Opposite below:
A woodland road on Bodmin Moor.

The personality of Jud Paynter, though I have no memory of where his name came from, was a complicated mixture of three men I knew, one Lancastrian, two Cornish. From the first came his comic pessimism – comic, that was, to me – from the second his drunkenness and his appearance, from the third his obstinacy, a sublime ability to mispronounce words, and his doom-laden religiosity. I used sometimes to see the second man on his nightly pilgrimage to his local pub. As his cottage was only a couple of hundred yards distant I could never understand why he bothered to use his bicycle. That is, until I saw him going home one night and realized that he used his bicycle to lean on.

It was this man's sister, with whom he lived, who became the prototype of Prudie.

I have sometimes wondered if the character of Jud Paynter in the books was not perhaps a bit over-coloured. Then while filming at Roscarrock I met him all over again: alive and well in 1977. On one occasion there I was being interviewed by two overseas journalists when the reincarnated Jud turned

up. The interview was totally swamped because 'Jud' launched into a monologue of his experiences which brooked no interruption. I was fascinated listening to the voice, observing the grimaces, the almost toothless gums, the ragged clothes, the battered hat that was now and then taken off so that a dirty thumb nail could scratch the bald head; but I'm not sure the journalists quite appreciated the joke. When they had finally walked off defeated, 'Jud' glanced after them disapprovingly, then screwed up his eyes at me and said: "Ow 'bout that, then!'

But he had no comic sense of triumph; he was only affronted that two of his audience had slipped away before he had finished.

★　★　★

The inland towns of Cornwall have not a great deal to recommend them. They are for the most part of granite, put up to fulfil a purpose and built to last. There was seldom money for decoration or embellishment – anyway granite is not an easy stone to work – but they grew as they were needed, straggling beside a few narrow roads, spreading out laterally, fluctuating in size with population and prosperity.

Launceston by its dominating position, its ancient castle, its mediaeval walls and its quite remarkable church is much the most interesting, and should be exempted from the above generalization.

Truro is the other exception. Built about the confluence of the Kenwyn and Allen rivers as they bubble down to meet the Fal, it became from about the middle of the eighteenth century to the middle of the nineteenth a winter centre for the neighbouring gentry. They had town houses there, and attended receptions, whistdrives and balls. It had an excellent little theatre, a Philharmonic Society which gave thirty concerts a year, a cricket club, a lending library, an elegant and ancient church. Many good houses were put up. Some are still there.

Then in 1880 it was decided that a cathedral should be built and a well-known architect, J. L. Pearson, was commissioned to design it. The present building was put up between 1898 and 1910. Granite from Mabe, granite from St Stephens, stone dressings from Corsham and Bath, slate from Delabole, serpentine from the Lizard, this cathedral was not designed like Exeter or Salisbury with green lawns and silent cloisters to distance itself from the merchandising and the traffic; it was intended to exist in the very heart of the town, to be a central eminence round which all the other buildings

Opposite:
The entrance to Launceston Castle.

Walsingham Place, Truro—saved from demolition by public protest.

clustered, as in Beauvais, Chartres, Rouen. Its style, early English Gothic, has been criticized by purists as an anachronism – like someone writing a Beethoven symphony today. One might wish that someone could do that also and do it as well. Pearson did it as well. The cathedral dominated the town, as intended, and existed in harmony with its surroundings. It at once made Truro a special place, a cut above everything else in the county. An aunt of mine, seeing it for the first time, said: 'What has this little town done to deserve such a beautiful building?'

About fifteen years ago I was asked by a magazine to write an article on the subject of 'My Favourite Town'. I chose Truro, for I have a deep and abiding affection for it. I would choose it no longer.

Somewhere around 1968 or a little earlier the City Fathers, or the business community within the Council, or whoever was the ultimate governing body, began to have grandiose visions for the little town. It should become the Mecca of the South West, and to this end no pains – and no buildings – should be spared. After the horrible demolition of the Red Lion Hotel the council seemed to develop a sort of dementia praecox of the aesthetic sensibilities, and abandoned everything to the planners and the modern architects. We have all seen particularly ugly examples of modern architecture: concrete boxes which look like the work of maimed men who have hurriedly assembled utility shelters at the end of an atomic war – and Truro now has many such examples. Some of the most unedifying cluster in the vicinity of the cathedral, making a peculiarly depressing sight for anyone who knew the old town before.

Of course this is happening, or has happened, in towns and cities all over England, and of course one cannot halt progress, and shouldn't wish to if it is discreetly managed. But it does seem to me a confession of aesthetic and conceptual failure if Cornwall can only achieve a centralization of its business and administrative offices by hacking out the heart and destroying the character of its one main town and only city.

★ ★ ★

When I knew Truro first, and for long after, it was possible to buy Evil Eye Pills at the chemist, for farmers who believed some animal of theirs had been ill-wished by a spiteful neighbour.

When I knew Truro first, and for long after, bubbling rills of water ran in the streets, between the street proper and the pavement. Scarcely a foot wide and only a few inches deep – varying of course with the season – these rivulets always seemed clean and fresh and added a special charm to the city. It's a pity they've had to go underground. I remember once driving in with my mother, her three-year-old grandson sitting on her knee. My son was a singularly equable child, contented and easy to please; but once in a rare while he had a bad day, and this was a bad day. He had grizzled and wriggled all the way in. I stopped in Boscawen Street and opened my door to get out. My mother also opened her door, whereupon my son picked up her new white gloves and hurled them out of the car. They settled happily into the rivulet and began their long bobbing journey towards the River Fal.

My tendency as a father was always to spare the rod, and this was no exception, but, having dashed after the gloves and saved them, I brought them dripping back to the car intent on expressing myself vigorously to the child. As I got back an elderly rosy-cheeked Cornishwoman was beaming in at the door of the car at my son. '*Dear* of 'n!' she said. 'Edn ee *love-ly*! . . . God's little messenger!'

So that afternoon God's little messenger didn't even get a wigging.

★　★　★

*A*nother town of which one might make an exception is Helston. Not for architectural excellence but because of the Furry Dance which takes place there on the first Saturday in May, and has done for some fourteen hundred years. Having grown through, as it were, the picturesque view of Cornwall, I for a long time leaned over backwards to avoid those things in Cornwall of particular attraction to the conventional tourist. So it was years before I was eventually persuaded by a Helston lady to share her window overlooking the main street. Of course it is a show. Of course it is self-conscious. Of course it is a tourist attraction. But under it all there is a deep sense of pagan ritual which continues to pervade the dance – and fascinates, and sometimes hypnotizes. The band plays the tune with endless repetition – only about sixteen notes in all – as an early nineteenth-century newspaper put it: music of more antiquity than variety. (The writer of the song based on this dance got it nearly right, but in a sense not *nearly* right.) The band guards its score jealously. There is more in this music than meets the ear. On the surface it is a charming celebration of summer. Below the surface it is very ancient and very earth-bound and rather haunted.

The same is true of the Padstow Hobby Horse, which in a way is a rougher celebration of the same May revels. I have never seen it, but a large group of the Poldark players went together; and they were impressed in the same way.

Above:
The front of Roscarrock—used in the second series for the opening
picture
where Ross and Demelza greeted one another.

Opposite:
Carbis Bay. This is where the television crew stayed
during the making of the first series.

Television Poldark

*I*t may or may not have been noticed that in writing of the television series I have had rather more to say about the second series than the first. This is because I had very much more to do with it.

*W*hen London Films took an option on the first four novels, I asked for, and received from them, an assurance that in any production they sponsored or undertook, the stories – and the style of the stories – should not be changed. At this stage it was not known who would make the films or how they would be made. An American-owned company was interested for a time. But when it was known that the BBC had contracted to do them, any doubts I might have had completely vanished. The people who had given me so much joy with their classic serials could do no wrong.

Even an aside from the producer when we were looking for sites in Cornwall that 'I hope you understand we have to make some changes,' did not alert me. I told him I had had six novels made into films and was hardened to such things.

But when they somewhat reluctantly let me see the first two scripts – which was obligatory under the terms of the contract – the happy camaraderie abated.

It has always been my principle to offer no public criticism or comment on any film or television play taken from my books because, though I would fight tooth and nail to prevent anyone altering a single comma in the books without explicit permission, where a translation into a new medium occurs there *have* to be alterations, a professional writer sells his work knowing very well there are going to be alterations, and it is bad manners and unprofessional to complain if the result is for some reason displeasing to him. It is not the author who is risking a million pounds (or whatever). His reputation may be a little on the line, but nothing like so much as that of the producer and director. He stands to lose nothing financially; other people do. So let them get on with it, and if good intentions may sometimes pave the road to Hell, no one in his right mind can suppose that the intention was not good from the start. People don't rise high in the film or television world and then carelessly or stupidly or wantonly cast their reputations away.

So, true to this principle, I'll say no more here – except that a lot of dust flew. Nevertheless, looking back on it all now, I am still startled by the bad quality of some of the early scripts. It is all the more surprising when one contrasts it with the scrupulous and loving attention to detail of the BBC technical staff when a film finally goes into production. Nothing is too much trouble to get things absolutely accurate as to time and place. Every set is correct to the smallest detail and costumes are always true to the time. Wander into a set just before the shooting: pick up a newspaper; it is sure to be a genuine one and about the right date. Details which the camera cannot possibly pick up are still observed, as if to create an atmosphere into which actors and directors can absorb themselves in a splendid illusion of reality, so that it may be passed on to the watching millions.

Sometimes the passion for accuracy almost goes too far. On one occasion a whole morning's work was re-shot the following day because it was discovered that Ross Poldark as an officer in the army had been wearing his peaked hat nose to nape, like Wellington, whereas before 1800 it should have been worn ear to ear, like Napoleon.

In the gardens of Lanhydrock Demelza and Hugh Armitage walked together at the beginning of their ill-fated love affair. They were photographed against a massive bank of flowering rhododendrons. I kept my fingers crossed, held my breath, and hoped no research girl with the company would discover that rhododendrons of that colour and size were not growing in England at the end of the eighteenth century. All, as it happened, was well.

Indifferent scripting is not of course confined to the first few episodes of *Poldark*, nor to the BBC. Perhaps it is an endemic risk in the very process of adaptation. Some authors, especially classical authors, do not write dialogue that will speak easily. Inevitably exigencies of screen time and production mean there have to be alterations in events, plot structure, story line. Some script writers, I think, read a novel a couple of times, then put it away before they begin their adaptation. One of the Poldark script writers, I know, did not bother to read the novel preceding the one he was asked to adapt. Perhaps they feel they have to put a more personal impression upon their work.

Opposite above:
The back of Roscarrock—the scene of Sawle Fair in the BBC television series.

Opposite below:
Roscarrock—the house that Ross gave to Demelza's two brothers to renovate in the second BBC television series.

The wall at Roscarrock where Ross was taken out to be shot.

But it need not be unsympathetically or carelessly written. Just as the first four episodes of the first series were very bad, so the last four of the second series, by Martin Worth, were a model of how it can be done.

There was a considerable improvement in the quality of the scripts as the first series went along, and – apart from the last episode of this series, when everything went haywire again – they kept pretty closely to the books. By then the producer's feeling for me – and mine for him – was not of the friendliest, and I saw nothing of the earlier shooting. So it was not until the production was half done that one day in my club I saw a good-looking young man who was describing how he had spent all morning drowning in a tank of water and I went across to him and said: 'Aren't you Clive Francis?' He said he was. Rather hesitantly I introduced myself, whereupon he put his arms around me and said, 'But why haven't you been to *see* us? We thought you didn't *like* us!' '*Like* you?' I said. 'I like and admire you all!'

Which was the truth. Whatever the shortcomings of the production team, it did not extend to their casting. Some of it was inspired. Where it was not inspired, or ran contrary to the physical description in the book, the actor or actress was strong enough to create a convincing role for himself or herself that satisfied in its own right.

The second series came about in a very different way. When it became clear that Poldark One had been such a great success the BBC sent down one of their producers, a very down-to-earth, good tempered, charming Australian, to see what had been wrong between us and how I felt about a second series, for which there was already in existence *The Black Moon* and a not-yet-published novel called *The Four Swans*. A third novel, not even started, was needed to complete a new trilogy. I expressed myself in no uncertain terms, as to my delight in the overall success of the series, and my dislike as to the way it had all begun.

He seemed to appreciate my frankness as much as I did his. Thereafter followed a meeting in London with an executive producer who, although connected with the first series, seemed unaware of a good deal that had been going on. He expressed courteous surprise and dismay; I made certain courteous conditions for the production of a second series, which he courteously accepted. We all carried out our parts, and there was no more trouble.

Not to be outdone, London Films made me their representative for the second series, so I stayed with the production all through.

The BBC at this stage were also singularly tactful in their attitude towards *The Angry Tide*, the third and final novel of the second series, which was only just begun. I told them nothing of the story line, and they asked nothing while it was being written. Only now and again an inquiry would come from the casting director, who would ring up and say, 'Actor X's contract comes up for renewal next week. Can you tell us whether he will be needed in the final four instalments?'

My wife and I came to know all the actors and technicians well, and they us. It even seemed sometimes as if they looked on us as lucky mascots and didn't feel it would go as well if we were not there. Certainly I came to have a great admiration for them all. It was a happy unit, welded by good-will and professional pride. Several actors said they had never before been with such a jolly group. For me the frustrations of '75 gave way to the fulfilments of '77, and it became a wonderful year.

Whether all this made much difference to the general viewer I do not know. It certainly made a great deal of difference to my feeling for the whole production.(It also proved that my own dialogue, where used, was as speakable as anyone else's.)

Lundy Bay. Scene of one of the shipwrecks in the first BBC television series.

Obviously a first series has all the impact, the 'attack' of a new thing; a second series is a follow-up. But at least the viewing figures stayed up and generally increased. For the final episode of the second series, which was played in competition against a Royal Command Performance with Bob Hope as compere on the ITV Channel, more than twelve million viewers stayed faithful to *Poldark*.

I do not know the exact proportion but I guess about a quarter of the total production was shot on location, the rest in the studios. I do not know by how much the location work influenced the total appeal; but clearly a very great deal. Not only did the characters gain people's fascinated attention but the land in which they lived and had their being. As a result of the series thousands of people have come to Cornwall from all over the world to see it for themselves. When I die and go to Heaven I shall not mention to St Peter that I wrote the Poldarks, for if he is a Cornishman – as I suspect – the chances are I shall be refused admittance for having caused even more 'foreigners' to invade his once quiet land.

The BBC very much wanted to do a third series, preferably to be ready for the following autumn. Nothing would have pleased me more, but I had to refuse because, however one judges the books, they are organic, character leading to action, action leading to a further development of character. To have written thirteen instalments, even in collaboration with a good and sympathetic script-writer, would have introduced a new element of haste and contrivance into the series. Apart from the public, it would somehow have been letting down the fictional people about whom I have come to care so much.

Opposite:
The farmyard at Roscarrock.

Above:
Trevelgue Head. An iron-age fort near Newquay.

Opposite:
The author on the beach at Porth Joke.

Postscript

A good many years ago when I was in Ibiza I met a young
American who told me he had just written a novel, and
would I read it and tell him what I thought? Heart sinking, I
agreed to do this – the sort of task any author jumps at while
on holiday – but to my surprise the MS was very well written,
and I later sent it to my US publisher with a strong letter of
recommendation. Asked by the author for a more detailed
opinion, I made a few small criticisms and one somewhat
larger one. In the story four young people are closeted
together in a New York heat wave. Presently two leave, and
within half an hour the other two are in bed together. I said: 'I
don't find your main character particularly likeable, in that he
should apparently so casually sleep with the wife of his best
and oldest friend.' A look came across the young author's face
– I can only call it a pitying look – making me feel as if I'd
emerged from some cloud-cuckooland of yesteryear which
had disappeared with the bow and arrow. I was forty-two at
the time.

But of course it is not just age that counts; it's the way one
looks at life, an attitude of mind, and most of all an attitude of
mind towards one's own experience. Hard as it may be for
cynics to believe, my personal experience on the whole has
been worthwhile and rewarding. Sex to me is one of the best
things in life, and love one of the most enduring. Men – and
women – have treated me well. I have never been betrayed or
let down by anyone important to me. I have never in my life
had to ask a favour of anyone, and therefore have never known
the bitterness of being refused or – so I'm told – the
resentment of being granted it. This does not mean I have not
known sadness and disappointment, ill health or the chagrins
of failure. Nor does it mean that I am full of the milk of human
kindness or that I believe human beings to be more admirable

than they really are; but it may just explain why the characters in *Poldark* are, if one balances the coin, a little more in the sun than in the shadow. As far as critical acceptance goes, this has been of great detriment. J. B. Priestley once said that practically all the substantial reputations of his time had been made by writers who appeared to be inspired by their gall bladders.

Theirs may of course be a truer picture of life. Who am I, who have lived only one life, to say? It can well be argued that marriages don't last – at least amicably. Some men do no doubt unhesitatingly sleep with the wives of their best friends. If you can cheat yourself to the top, do you not do so? Who is honest any more, it may be said? Or ever was? One does not need to go to the bestialities of the concentration camp and the political prison to be able to argue that man is a contemptible animal.

But surely one must still judge by personal experience, not by the experience of others, not by the mood of the time. Some happiness, and that which is identifiable as good, flourishes in the world in spite of evil, even if it is less newsworthy, harder to write about, and less fashionable. As the newspaper man said: 'One rape is worth ten golden weddings.' It is the business of the novelist – or should be – to show both sides. Some great novelists have. If in the Poldarks I have tended to show too much of the warmer side, that is my own fault – or my own truth.

★ ★ ★

*T*his summer I walked along the beach of Porth Joke. It was in the middle of a spell of bad weather, but a golden day had slipped in in spite of the forecasts. It was evening, and the few people who had been there during the day had gone. There was no wind. The sea was quiet. The sun was two hand spaces from the horizon. The sand ripples were as regular as lines in a child's exercise book. Barley and wheat were ripening in the sloping fields nearby. When I have to take permanent leave of Cornwall I shall wish it to be on such an evening as this. *Atque in perpetuum, frater, ave atque vale . . .*

But next summer perhaps the sun will be shining again.

★ ★ ★

The North Coast above Boscastle near Crackington Haven.

Above:
The author walking along the cliff
path at Porth Joke.

List of Illustrations

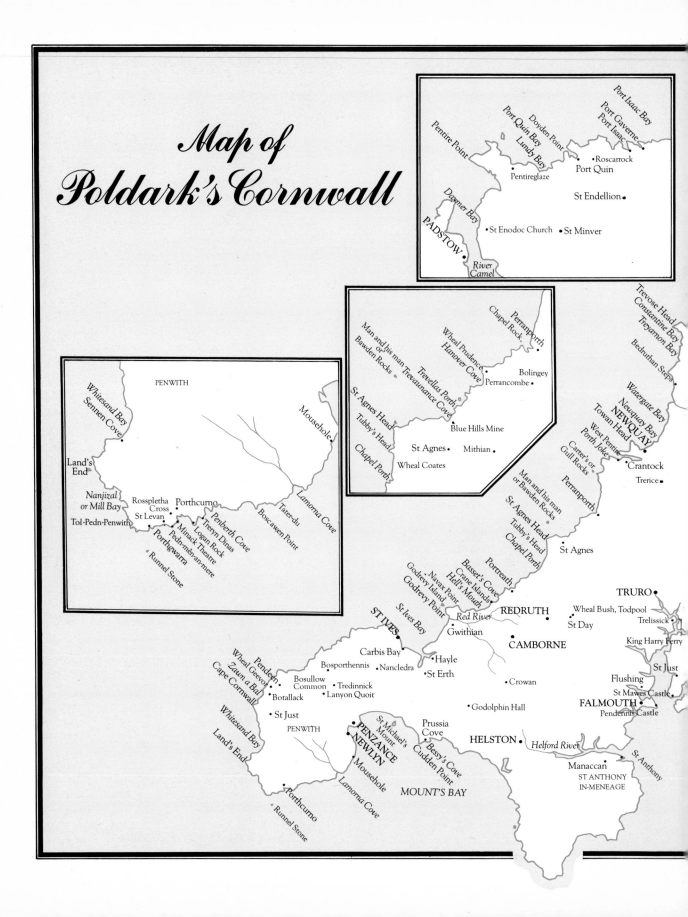

Map of Poldark's Cornwall

BUDE
Widemouth Bay
Penhalt Cliff
Crackington Haven
Samphire Rock
The Strangles
Voter Run
Rusey Beach
High Cliff
Boscastle
Beeny Cliff
Tintagel Head
Tintagel
Port Gaverne
Port Isaac
Delabole
LAUNCESTON
Altarnun
Pentire Point
Port Quin
Lewannick
Polzeath Bay
PADSTOW
St Endellion
St Minver
BODMIN MOOR
River Camel
River Tamar
MAWGAN-IN-PYDAR
St Mawgan
Warleggan
Lanherne Valley
BODMIN
Lanhydrock House
River Fowey
Demelza
Goss Moor
Boconnoc
Roche
Tregays
River Lerryn
St Winnow
River Fal
ST AUSTELL
FOWEY
PLYMOUTH
Tregony
CUBY
Bessie Beneath
Caerhays Castle
Porthluney Cove
Portholland
ST JUST-IN-ROSELAND
Portscatho

Map by Peter Wrigley

ACKNOWLEDGEMENT

*I would like to thank Fred L. Harris
for his general advice and for having
a friendly finger in this pie, as he
has had in most pies I have cooked
for Cornwall.*